BLACK HEARTS AND PAINTED GUNS

BLACK HEARTS AND PAINTED GUNS

A Battalion's Journey into Iraq's Triangle of Death

By

KELLY EADS AND DANIEL S. MORGAN

CASEMATE

Pennsylvania & Yorkshire

AN AUSA BOOK
Association of the United States Army
2425 Wilson Boulevard, Arlington, Virginia, 22201, USA

First published in the United States of America and Great Britain in 2023.
Reprinted as a paperback in 2025 by
CASEMATE PUBLISHERS
1950 Lawrence Road, Havertown, PA 19083, USA
and
47 Church Street, Barnsley, S70 2AS, UK

Paperback Edition: ISBN 978-1-63624-534-8
Digital Edition: ISBN 978-1-63624-198-2

A CIP record for this book is available from the British Library

Printed and bound in the United Kingdom by CPI Group (UK) Ltd, Croydon, CR0 4YY
Typeset in India by Lapiz Digital Services, Chennai.

For a complete list of Casemate titles, please contact:

CASEMATE PUBLISHERS (US)
Telephone (610) 853-9131
Fax (610) 853-9146
Email: casemate@casematepublishers.com
www.casematepublishers.com

CASEMATE PUBLISHERS (UK)
Telephone (0)1226 734350
Email: casemate@casemateuk.com
www.casemateuk.com

The Publisher's authorised representative in the EU for product safety is Authorised Rep Compliance Ltd., Ground Floor, 71 Lower Baggot Street, Dublin D02 P593, Ireland.
http://www.arccompliance.com

This book is dedicated to

All those warriors and families who fought and died defending our beloved nation. Especially to those from 2nd Battalion, 502nd Infantry Regiment, 101st Airborne (Air Assault). Your sacrifice and friendship will never be forgotten

and

Alpha Company 2-502, 101st Airborne SFC Jonathan Tessar; SPC Justin Byler; PFC David Martin; and PFC Adam Johnson KIA 10-31-2005

"We few, we happy few. We band of brothers!"

Henry V, Act IV,
William Shakespeare

"Blessed are the peacemakers, for they shall be called sons of God."

Matthew 5:9

"When it comes your time to die, be not like those whose hearts are filled with the fear of death, so that when their time comes, they weep and pray for a little more time to live their lives over again in a different way. Sing your death song and die like a hero going home."

Chief Tecumseh, Shawnee Nation

Contents

Acknowledgements

First, and most important, we would like to thank Almighty God for his plan to bring these stories forward and allow us to share them with you. We are grateful to Him for blessing this nation, our military, and the 101st Airborne Division (Air Assault)—the historic "Screaming Eagles."

Second, we want to thank our Fallen Heroes. This story expresses the deep admiration for their devotion to duty, units, fellow warriors, and the United States of America. Their stories are not about politics. They are about a bond of commitment to each other during extreme situations beyond their control. Their call was to service and to each other. Their sacrifice deserves a story so that both their families and friends can get a glimpse of what their loved ones endured in combat, but also understand how brave and loved they were by their leaders, subordinates, and peers. We were a band of brothers.

For those of you who have lost a loved one during the Global War on Terror, our thoughts remain with you. We do not know God's plan, but one thing we can tell you is that we fought faraway against evil to prevent terrorism from ever reaching America as it did on 9/11. We thank you for supporting and loving our troops. It was our honor to serve with them.

Third, we want to thank the leadership of 2nd Battalion, 502nd Infantry Regiment for providing documents and insights for this book. Their patience and commitment to its writing was instrumental in helping tell the stories accurately, learning about other perspectives in battle, how the decisions were made by leaders, and helping us remember things that we, as authors, buried deep in our memory.

We would like to recognize those who served with us who provided intimate details, whether horrific, sad or humorous, that helped bring these stories back to life: Captain Baldwin, Sergeant First Class Geleney, Staff Sergeant Morgan, Staff Sergeant Skurzewski, Staff Sergeant Crispin, Staff Sergeant Girard, Staff Sergeant Mora, Sergeant Calhoun (3rd ID), Specialist Stoch, Specialist Hursey, Specialist Sawyer, Specialist Stauch, and Specialist Ables. Their openness enabled us to recognize those who went far beyond expectations to serve this country and protect fellow soldiers. It has taken years for us to come to grips with writing portions of this book. The research and putting words on paper, although painful at times, helped refresh our own recollection of events that faded with time.

Last, but not least, we want to thank family and friends who encouraged us through tough times during war. Most war stories dismiss or ignore what we call the kitchen table battlefield. Families manage so much while their loved ones are deployed in combat. The efforts that families endure are not as glorious or exciting as combat stories, but they are the foundation of the well-being of any unit and their soldier. Our families have watched over us, often late at night, constantly on the computer trying to get facts and feelings onto paper. Without family and friends, this book would not have been possible.

We also owe a shout-out to America's youth. Post-9/11 warriors volunteered and set aside an early part of their young adulthood to serve this country in war. No generation has been asked to serve in combat zones for such an extended period of time. Soldiers and their families had been on constant rotation since 2001 through 2021 when missions in Afghanistan and Iraq effectively ended. Regardless, this generation continues to adapt and deploy against emerging threats, such as Russian aggression against Ukraine. They recognize the need to serve and step forward, which speaks volumes about their character and devotion to protect our nation.

We believe that our nation's youth is not lost or misguided like many say. They step up and fight when America needs them; they are the nation's sons and daughters. Americans, regardless of the generation, have fought and will fight at the highest caliber against all enemies. The famed 101st, known as "The Band of Brothers," have fought day in and day out since World War II to ensure nothing less than victory and freedom of democracy around the world are maintained and attained. Our modern-day Screaming Eagles answered the call after the nation was attacked by terrorists on 9/11, put everything on the line to protect and preserve our sacred homeland, and performed as those in their lineage would demand and expect.

Military Terms and Ranks

AAR	After Action Review
AO	Area of Operation
AQI	Al-Qaeda in Iraq
AQIZ	Zarqawi's close network of AQI cell members
BDA	Battlefield Damage Assessment
BFV	Bradley Fighting Vehicle
BIAP	Baghdad International Airport
BN	Battalion
BDE	Brigade
CAG	Combat Applications Group (Delta Force)
Chalk	A group of airborne soldiers that deploy from one aircraft
CJTF	Command Joint Task Force
CO	Commanding Officer
CQB	Close Quarter Battle
CT	Counterterrorism
DIV	Division
DUSTWUN	Duty Status Whereabouts Unknown
EFP	Energy Formed Projectile
EKIA	Enemy Killed in Action
EOD	Explosive Ordnance Device
ERT	Emergency Response Team
EFP	Explosively Formed Penetrator
FOB	Forward Operating Base
GWOT	Global War on Terror
HBIED	House-Borne Improvised Explosion Device

HEDP	High-Explosive Dual-Purpose grenade
HMMWV	High-Mobility Multipurpose Wheeled Vehicle ("Humvee")
HVT	High-Value Target
HQ	Headquarters
ID	Infantry Division
IED	Improvised Explosive Device
ISF	Iraqi Security Forces
ISIS	Islamic State of Iraq and Syria
ISR	Intelligence, Surveillance, Reconnaissance
JAM	Jaysh al-Mahdi
KIA	Killed in Action
LD	Line of Departure
LOC	Line of Communication
LZ	Landing Zone
MAS	Muqtada al-Sadr
Medevac	Medical Evacuation
MOB	Man Overboard
MRE	Meal, Ready-to-Eat
NCO	Non-Commissioned Officer
NCOIC	Non-Commissioned Officer in Charge
NFA	No Fire Area
OBL	Osama bin Laden
OP	Observation Post
PCC	Pre-Combat Check
PCI	Pre-Combat Inspection
PRC	Portable Radio Communications
PZ	Pickup Zone
QRF	Quick Reaction Force
RCIED	Remote-Controlled Improvised Explosive Device
RECONDO	Reconnaissance Commando and Doughboy
ROE	Rules of Engagement
RPG	Rocket-Propelled Grenade
RPK	Ruchnoy Pulemyot Kalashnikova, a Russian light machine gun

RTO	Radio Telephone Operator
SAM	Surface-to-Air Missile
SAS	Special Air Service
SAW	Squad Automatic Weapon
Serial	A group of people, vehicles, or equipment
SF	Special Forces
SLLS	Stop, Look, Listen, Smell
SKT	Small Kill Team
SOCOM	Special Operations Command
SOI	Sons of Iraq
SOF	Special Operation Forces
TAC	Tactical Assault Command
TIC	Troops in Contact
TST	Time-Sensitive Target
UAH	Up-Armored High-Mobility Multipurpose Wheeled Vehicle
UAV	Unmanned Aerial Vehicle
VBIED	Vehicle-Borne Improvised Explosive Device
VOIED	Victim-Operated Improvised Explosive Device
WIA	Wounded in Action
XO	Executive Officer

Ranks

PVT	Private
PFC	Private First Class
SPC	Specialist
CPL	Corporal
SGT	Sergeant
SSG	Staff Sergeant
SFC	Sergeant First Class
1SG	First Sergeant
SM	Sergeant Major
CSM	Command Sergeant Major
1LT	First Lieutenant

2LT	Second Lieutenant
CPT	Captain
MAJ	Major
LTC	Lieutenant Colonel
COL	Colonel
BG	Brigadier General
MG	Major General
LTG	Lieutenant General
GEN	General

Preface

This book describes the valor and selflessness of America's warfighters in 2nd Battalion, 502nd Infantry Regiment, 101st Airborne Division (Air Assault), or "Strike Force." Much of this book is focused on my deployment with this historic regiment, 2005–2007, in Iraq where I had the privilege fighting with this battalion against radical Islamists. I hope that this book serves as a reminder to our fellow Americans, veterans, families, and leaders alike—of who we were, what we felt, how we fought, and how we survived.

I started to write this story as a personal tribute to my fellow Strike Force soldiers. It took some courage to revisit this time. In early 2020, I reconnected with recently retired Colonel Dan Morgan, who was our operations officer during my first deployment with the battalion in 2005–2006. Dan and I linked up through social media. It had been years since we had spoken with each other. As combat veterans with shared experiences, however, time is not a factor. We picked up our relationship like no time had passed between us.

Dan asked how and what I was doing. He informed me that he felt he had failed himself and former soldiers by not staying in touch. He realized by staying connected he was helping his family and him in transition and hopefully other veterans. I mentioned that I was gathering facts and writing a book about our deployment. Numerous soldiers had already assisted me in this task, but I knew there was much more to be told. He chimed in at the right time and right place, which resulted in a major boost in the details for the book. Dan was an aggressive combat officer who thrived in those combat environments. Little did he realize back then that combat became his personality and comfort zone. The

Army deployed him back-to-back every other year for over two decades. He retired from the Army in 2018 and fate pulled us back together in 2020. We dove full force together into this book.

I shared the rough manuscript with him. Dan had more one-year-plus deployments than any other officer I knew and had spent half of his children's lives in and out of combat. He is also an author and has been published on defense matters and leadership many times. He was generous in providing more details and the much-needed context from a battalion leadership perspective. His work made the book much stronger, so I asked him to coauthor the book with me.

The primary voice of the book is mine. Dan enters the story as himself, then a major and my operations officer during my first deployment. I have been able to portray him and his interactions with other leaders and the men due to his efforts to recreate the situations and conversations of the time. He drops out of the story for my other deployment to Iraq from the fall of 2007 to the winter of 2008 as he was deployed multiple times with other units. However, his help in researching and helping me get the details of the operations right was invaluable.

Going to war and conducting violence to break your enemy's will to fight is like no other experience. The anxiety that builds up in you as a warrior is by turns frightening and exhilarating. Your whole life becomes vivid. As a leader, you need to know your soldiers and do everything you can to have the will to lead in combat to the best of your ability. You concern yourself with whether you trained your unit enough. Each day revolves around mission, your unit, and execution of controlled violence. On every mission, it's as if you are leaving everything you hold dear, realizing that you may not see your family again. You force yourself not to be overcome with emotions over this separation. It's tough, but as a leader, you must come to grips with it, and lead with physical and moral courage. It is a complex, psychological balance of character, grit, empathy, and fear.

You are in a faraway land in a strange culture fighting an enemy who only wants to kill as many of your comrades-in-arms as possible, while at the same time you are holding together your unit under stress. Your warriors are human beings, hunting and killing other human beings.

Over time, you begin to realize that with the mission you focus on winning on the battlefield because if you do not win, your warriors will die. Tactical, visible leadership that fearlessly shares the hardships on the battlefield with the soldiers is paramount to build trust and loyalty in the command unit. From our battalion commander, Lieutenant Colonel Rob Haycock and down to the teams, our leaders possessed the physical courage needed to build trust and loyalty. True combat leaders give of themselves to plan, coordinate, and execute the mission to protect their unit; nothing means more to unit success and well-being.

America was at war for two decades in Afghanistan and Iraq, the longest war in our nation's history. This war took a toll on generations of warriors. Some of us have children born after 9/11 who fought an enemy on the same lands that, we their parents, fought twenty years ago. Although the commitment of multi-generational military families is admirable, the seemingly endless duration of the war created "compassion fatigue" within our ranks and in our citizens.

Compassion fatigue is an indifference by leadership and others to the suffering and sacrifice of those fighting for freedom. Since the early 2000s, America has watched thousands of news stories and read hundreds of accounts of combat. Numerous Hollywood movies have been produced depicting aspects of this war. Some of these movies are authentic and meaningful, but many more mostly glorify war. It is important for the media to make the public aware of the triumphs and horrors of war.

Despite all the coverage, the effect of decades of war on the dedicated warriors themselves is not fully understood or as well known by society. Combat veterans and their families have to fight compassion fatigue and the separation from normalcy. Many have deployed and redeployed so many times that each time it gets harder to maintain belief in the mission. Leaders struggle to motivate their warriors daily in combat. People say insanity is doing the same thing over and over but expecting a different result. Each deployment results in more committed warriors killed in action. Each Fallen Hero is a son, daughter, husband, wife, father, mother, brother, or sister. Over the years of war, each casualty leads to numbness of their service and a loss of perspective in the value of human life. Compassion fatigue basically leads to becoming disconnected to the suffering of others. We fought this every day in hostile terrain. The only thing that was predictable was that we would engage with the enemy and that we would suffer casualties at some point. It was just a question of how horrific and how many.

During my two deployments, our battalion experienced thousands of Improvised Explosive Device (IED) detonations and firefights. Some of these IED strikes were multiple 500-pound aviation bombs. We spent three months executing a counter-sniper fight that resulted in many fellow warriors being killed or wounded. We spent countless hours in blistering 120 degree heat, while controlling roads and preventing enemy freedom of movement. We spent months hunting enemy mortar teams, financial supporters, hit squads, bomb makers, and terror cell leadership, while protecting the locals in such an ambiguous environment. This led to physical and emotional exhaustion with feelings of self-contempt, irritability, and outright hatred of the enemy and occasionally the local population. It is a story that needs to be told.

In sharing the exploits and courage of the 2-502nd "Strike Force," it is my hope that it can help fellow soldiers, families, and senior military and political leadership overcome the compassion fatigue that affects our military's well-being. As you read about the journey of the Strike Force men and women you will recognize the bravery, selflessness, and camaraderie of these warriors, despite a harrowing number of combat incidents that occurred within a single infantry battalion.

The title of the book derives from the way the enemy perceived our unit. The first portion of the title, Black Hearts, originated from a black cloth heart placed on the side of our helmets. The heart distinguished the 502nd Infantry Regiment from other units on the battlefield. This symbol has been used since World War II and is accompanied by other 101st Airborne insignia, such as the spade, diamond, Rakkasan Tori and club. Our exploits and aggressive nature would lead the enemy to identify us as the Black Hearts.

The Painted Guns portion of the title comes from how the enemy described our Scout Platoon. The Scout Platoon painted and camouflaged their weapons to blend into the terrain in which they often conducted surveillance, reconnaissance, and ambush operations, patrolling deep into enemy territory, gathering intelligence, or targeting terror cell leadership. The enemy quickly identified this technique and the name stuck.

Most of the media coverage at the time focused on operations in the city of Baghdad proper, not the outskirts where we were fighting an extremely brutal battle on a day-to-day basis. Early on, our leaders made the decision to take the fight directly to the enemy by setting up patrol bases in the local areas where he lived and operated. This strategy was unique to us. Living in a desert environment was tough, but it allowed us to keep the pressure on the targets. When General William Casey, the Commanding General for Multi-National Forces–Iraq, attended a ceremony for our unit, he remarked it was rare that he could point to a single unit that had had such a strategic impact on his two goals of securing Baghdad and defeating Al-Qaeda.

No matter what you may think of the political decisions to go to war or the morality of the war itself, this book is about inspiration, not politics. The real-life men and women who are part of this story as well as those who have served previously in the 101st Airborne inspired us to write this book. Coupled with the sacrifices of our families, it is about the courage, bravery, and commitment of our tightknit unit, fighting a battle-tested, violent group of Al-Qaeda fighters and other extremist groups during multiple deployments.

—K.E.

Prologue

The explosion shattered the stillness of a sunny fall day, cutting the road in half just yards in front of our truck.

Large pieces of the asphalt were plummeting from the sky like hail and bouncing off the trucks. It looked like a meteor shower out of some Hollywood movie. I could not locate my platoon leader who had just been standing right where the IED had detonated. There is no way he could have survived that blast.

An insanely loud ringing was going off in my ears as I pulled myself back up into the gun turret. I positioned myself behind the .50-caliber machine gun, looking for the enemy through a haze of dirt, debris, and smoke. They were nowhere in sight.

We had pushed our reconnaissance patrol right into the middle of an extremely well-coordinated ambush by Al-Qaeda fighters who were reportedly defending Abu Musab al-Zarqawi, the commander and leader of AQ in Iraq (AQI).

The entire area was covered in a haze of dirt. Soldiers screaming everywhere. Suddenly, another large IED exploded behind us, again effectively cutting the road, preventing us from maneuvering on enemy fighters or breaking contact. We were in a kill zone surrounded by an unseen enemy.

As I turned to look back towards the initial IED blast, I saw my lieutenant walk out of the dust and back onto the road to take over the fight. I could not believe he had survived—and without so much as a scratch.

We were consumed by enemy small-arms fire and trapped in a daisy chain of consecutive IED explosions. Our mounted element could not go forward or backwards due to the massive road craters from the IEDs. The platoon leader made contact with Major Dan Morgan, our operations officer, on the radio, who then began directing Apache AH-64 helicopters and unmanned aerial vehicles (UAVs) to the area.

★

In October 2005, the war in Iraq took an unexpected turn to sectarian violence between Iraq's Sunni and Shi'a population. The insurgency was at its all-time high due to foreign fighters flooding into Iraq to join the Sunni uprising against the Iraqi Shi'a majority and the United States. Musab al-Zarqawi called for a jihad to fight against the invaders and to maintain Sunni dominance. The region exploded into all-out war.

AQI seized a region in southwest Baghdad. The area possessed critical terrain because of the roads from Fallujah running along the Euphrates River and into south Baghdad. The area was tribal, farming land with a network of canals and roads—very similar to the hedgerow fight that followed in Normandy during World War II. U.S. forces were mostly focused on the city of Baghdad and building security for a stable government, while we were on the outskirts with minimal support.

This area between Yusifuyah, Mahmudiyah, and Iskandariyah, aka "The Triangle of Death," became a safe haven for leadership and resources. It was the primary mobility corridor for suicide bombers, especially vehicle-borne improvised explosive devices (VBIEDS). The region was a perfect place for AQI's headquarters. The palm groves, farm fields, and canals created a natural defense network that separated AQI elements from American forces. The terrain enabled early warning defenses and prevented freedom of movement and surprise rapid-ground assaults by U.S. forces. The area was also a perfect location to conduct unconventional, guerrilla-style attacks on U.S. and coalition forces in Baghdad. The multiple roadways running to and from Baghdad gave AQI the ability to move about freely and uncontested.

The past unit's mission was to protect the southern portion of Baghdad International Airport (BIAP), which they did quite well. This success led to minimal exploitation-like U.S. offensive operations into this countryside. A couple of ventures into the area in 2004–2005 were met with massive IEDs and well-coordinated ground attacks by AQI fighters.

So, the unit chose to consolidate its gains on the defense of BIAP, creating a safe haven that threatened Baghdad.

Unchallenged, AQI fortified the area with a protective belt of IEDs and early warning networks. They established a command-and-control node that facilitated the movement of their fighters, VBIEDs, weapons, finances, and other resources into Baghdad. They were in it for the long haul, confident that they were secure from ground attack, and could sow terror, division, and chaos in the city and its environs.

In 2003 and 2004, General David Petraeus had led the Black Hearts of 2nd Brigade, 502nd Infantry Regiment in its fight from Kuwait to Mosul, Iraq. During this time, Dan Morgan was a company commander in this urban fight. The Black Hearts, under Petraeus and Colonel Joe Anderson, had regained control of the city of Mosul in northern Iraq and demonstrated stellar combat capabilities and experience. In 2005, just a year later, the Strike Brigade was now tasked to do the same in southwest Baghdad. The U.S. Army and General William Casey, Commanding General Multi-National Forces–Iraq, chose the Black Hearts to take on the task.

Major Morgan, who had a relationship with General Petraeus, discussed the upcoming mission for our battalion. Morgan had barely settled at home with his family and was already getting ready for more combat. Petraeus informed him that the area was an enemy stronghold and held significant future value for the direction of the war against AQI, and to expect violence. The brigade would spearhead an operation that would drive directly into the heart of the Triangle of Death to disrupt AQI's freedom of movement, locate and dismantle known VBIED factories, and kill or capture AQI high-value targets (HVTs). The HVTs consisted of known persons associated with criminal and terror cells in the area attacking and killing both coalition forces and local citizens.

Intelligence suggested that the area of operations (AO) consisted of senior AQI leadership, financiers, bombmakers and battle-hardened AQI operatives. In addition, we expected a population who were passively and actively complicit in facilitating and assisting AQI. This is what we faced: a violent fight in a small region that would become a pivotal point in the war.

CHAPTER I

A Call to Serve

Most people over a certain age can remember where they were on September 11, 2001. Each has their own story about that day. Almost 20 years later, it's practically a cliché to call 9/11 the day when everything changed. But for the thousands of men and women who decided to join the U.S. military after the attack, it really did change everything. Those who were active duty were trained and ready. New recruits needed to be prepared as soon as possible. America never expected that the war against a determined enemy in multiple theaters would turn out to be the longest conflict in our history.

I grew up in a small Mid-Western town located in the northwestern portion of Missouri, about an hour north of Kansas City. I was 16 years old on the fateful day of 9/11. I was sitting in my classroom, in the first class of the day, Current Events, with my other classmates waiting for the teacher. Suddenly, she came running frantically into the room. Without saying a word, she quickly grabbed the remote on her desk and turned on the television at the front. As we watched the scenes of chaos unfolding, she told us the Twin Towers in New York City had been struck by an airliner. We all looked at each other. We had no idea what the Twin Towers were.

We saw replay footage of the first commercial jet plane crashing in a fiery inferno into one of two huge skyscrapers. As we watched, we saw live footage of another jet hit the second tower minutes later. The commentator said a third plane had slammed into the Pentagon and a fourth had crash-landed in a field in Somerset County, Pennsylvania.

While watching what appeared to be coordinated disasters, all of us were numb, unsure of what to say or do. But we knew one thing: America had been attacked. Our freedom was being threatened.

While growing up, I knew I would do two things with my life: serve in the military and become a police officer. If I could, I would have run away from school straight to a recruiter's office and signed up to serve and fight for our country right then and there. However, I was too young and it wasn't an option.

A couple days later, President George W. Bush, the 43rd President of the United States, guided our country out of shock, mobilizing people to recover and defend the nation. I'll never forget seeing President Bush standing in the rubble of the Twin Towers, and announce, while holding back tears and emotions, "Every nation, in every region, now has a decision to make. Either you are with us, or you are with the terrorists." Osama bin Laden and his terrorist cohorts had energized the greatest defender of democracy with more resources and the finest military than any other country in the world. The United States would be going to war.

I already knew I wanted to join the military and eventually law enforcement. I enjoyed an adrenaline-packed lifestyle as a kid and knew both of these careers would offer that excitement and purpose for me. Though I was focused and determined on getting into this fight, I found myself getting into trouble a lot too, seriously jeopardizing my chances. The natural need for adrenaline rushes resulted in some pretty dumb choices, such as fighting; paintballing, ironically, a police station; intentionally getting the local police officers riled while screaming through town on four-wheelers so they would chase us; driving way too fast; and getting hurt a lot doing other insanely stupid things to impress the girls.

More important, my parents raised me right. My behavior was my decision and not their fault. They had to have instilled a sense of service. I was blessed with their example and am seeing my son with the same traits. That same mentality is what I really believe fueled my passion to serve for a greater cause.

After the attacks, I was laser focused on my dream of joining the military. I became obsessed with the history of the 101st Airborne and

Ranger Regiment. I watched numerous movies and documentaries and read books about their storied profession. When I was old enough, I wanted to join either famous unit to become part of their history and serve among the most elite soldiers in the world.

I finally enlisted in the Army in the summer of 2003. I made it clear to the recruiter that I wanted to fight for my country on the front lines, despite his well-meaning suggestions for other noncombatant positions. My parents were very supportive of my desire to join the military. As many in my family had served before, however, neither parent was too fond of my wanting to be in the infantry and on the front lines. My mother sat back and listened, but my father really tried to suggest and inform my decision to choose a career field that would help me find a post-military career. Neither thought being a grunt on the front line was a career field nor beneficial for a career after the military.

Nevertheless, I quickly found myself signing a four-year contract with the United States Army as an infantryman, also known as an 11 Bravo. Before I knew it, I found myself on an airplane being flown to the U.S. Army's Fort Benning, Georgia, the home of the infantry. I was proud to serve alongside the absolute best our nation had to offer—men and women of the U.S. military.

Our basic training was happening right in the middle of two ongoing conflicts: Iraq and Afghanistan. The drill sergeants took training to a whole new level because they knew that when we graduated many of us would go straight into a combat zone. We were woken from our bunks late at night by drill sergeants screaming and forcing us to push our bodies to levels we had never experienced. They constantly challenged us with the physical and mental rigors of combat.

Right before graduation, I remember sitting in our barracks in the stifling Georgia heat. My fellow recruits and I had all put in our requests for unit assignments and were anxiously awaiting our orders. We were trained for combat, some would say brainwashed, and desperately wanted to fight in the Middle East. However, once the orders started to come down, many of us got deployed to South Korea. What the hell? I thought. We were at war in the Middle East not Asia. The reason was that since the troop requirements for Iraq and Afghanistan were so critical, the

Army was deploying veteran soldiers from South Korea to Iraq first, then replenishing the ranks in South Korea with new recruits.

We sweated out the process as our names were called. I just prepared myself for South Korea. Then the commissioning officer called out, "Eads. Fort Campbell, 101st Airborne Division (Air Assault)." I about jumped out of my skin. I was speechless. Thanks to Almighty God, I had gotten my first request to join the ranks of the 101st. As we say in the 101st Airborne Division "We, or I, had a rendezvous with destiny!" Fort Campbell, Kentucky, was the home to some of the most elite units in the Army, such as the 5th Special Forces Group, the 160th Special Operations Aviation Regiment, the Sabalauski Air Assault School, and the 101st Airborne Division (Air Assault,) and within that division, the 502nd Infantry Unit (Strike Force) which was the longest-serving regiment within the 101st since World War II.

CHAPTER 2

The Legacy of the 101st Airborne "Screaming Eagles"

The 101st Airborne Division (Air Assault) embodies the character and values of America's commitment to freedom. The 101st is considered the most lethal and tactically mobile unit in America's military arsenal. Its history on the battlefield is legendary.

The division was activated on August 16, 1942, at Camp Claiborne, Louisiana. In his first address to the 101st soldiers, General William C. Lee, said that though the division had no history, it did have a "rendezvous with destiny," and "the Division would be called on for the most extreme, challenging, and immediate missions." On June 6, 1944, D-Day, the Screaming Eagles became the first American unit to set foot in occupied France, on the Cotentin Peninsula during Operation *Overlord*.

Screaming Eagle soldiers jumped into Normandy just a couple hours prior to the main landings: more than 50,000 paratroopers jumped from the C-47 Sky Trains. Prior to the main body, the 101st paratroopers, along with members of the 82nd Airborne Division, inserted to seize a variety of objectives, such as roads, bridges, and villages. Basically, this meant that the Screaming Eagles needed to jump in at night, before dawn, and set the conditions to help the landing forces' assault onto the beaches and then into the Normandy hinterland.

During the operation, on June 6, one brave commander, Lieutenant Colonel Cole, leading 3rd Battalion, 502nd Infantry, parachuted and hit the ground and assembled approximately 75 men out of his 500-plus soldiers. The rest had been injured, captured, or lost. He then went on to capture an area just behind Utah beach where he and his men awaited the landing of the 4th Infantry Division. After completing their first mission, Cole's battalion was re-established and utilized to attack Carentan, a German stronghold. While moving towards the objective, the 502nd sustained major friendly force casualties from Allied bombing runs. Upon reaching the outskirts of Carentan, Cole encountered heavy German firepower. Knowing Carentan had to be taken, he ordered his men to fix bayonets and assault the German positions. The assault, later named "Cole's Charge," was successful and captured key territory that eventually led to the fall of Carentan, a major achievement for the 101st and U.S. Army in the early days of the invasion.

As the Allies fought their way inland, the 101st was called upon for numerous operations that were critical to the outcome of the war. What made the 101st Screaming Eagles special was their ability to respond quickly to senior leadership's mission objectives and requests. One of the historic battles that included the 101st occurred during the Battle of the Bulge, at Bastogne. The German December 1944 offensive to drive a wedge between the Allied armies and capture the critical port of Antwerp had taken the Allies by surprise and they were now in headlong retreat. The 101st was ordered to reinforce the inexperienced and demoralized U.S. troops at Bastogne, which now became the crucial hub in the Battle of the Bulge.

The 101st deployed from France after resting and refitting following the disastrous Operation *Market Garden* in Holland. They rapidly moved into the area of operations at Bastogne, setting up defensive positions to interdict and prevent further German advances on Bastogne. Eventually the Germans surrounded the 101st with overwhelming firepower, especially artillery; however, they could not forcibly remove the dug-in, gritty Screaming Eagles.

The 101st held the line for over 24 hours before it was eventually reinforced by General George Patton's Third Army. U.S. forces had blunted the attack which ultimately forced the Germans to retreat, and their offensive petered out. Eventually, increased offensive operations by Allied forces in the west and the Soviet Red Army in the east led to the defeat of Germany in May 1945. The defense of Bastogne broke the back of the Germans in the west and earned the 101st Airborne the first Presidential Unit Citation. It was the first citation ever issued to an entire division.

In 1958, General William Westmoreland took a decision to increase the lethality and expertise in small-team tactics within the 101st. He was a veteran of World War II and knew how important it was that small units separated from main elements could still attack and defeat a superior enemy. So, he created the 101st Airborne RECONDO School. The school focused on demolitions, the art of patrolling, intelligence-gathering, recognition of enemy vehicles, woodlands survival, land navigation, rappelling, firearm skills on all weapons, and aggressive hand-to-hand combat drills. The school developed a reputation for being physically and mentally demanding, regardless of rank or position.

The RECONDO patch is an arrowhead pointed downward. It is black and white, indicating that the soldier is skilled to conduct operations both day and night. The arrowhead pointing downward indicates assault from above. The RECONDO recognition set the 101st Airborne Division apart from other units. The patch remains etched in history where its design and purpose contributed to modern-day 101st patches with different designs and colors. When I arrived at the 101st in 2004, I saw the patch painted on walls and entryways in order to carry on the legacy and tradition of our RECONDO forefathers.

During the Vietnam War, the division transformed from an airborne unit to an air assault unit, known then as air mobile. The terrain in Vietnam demanded mobility of units to be able to rapidly deploy to specific locations in order to surround and assault enemy forces. The use of highly mobile helicopters was the answer to this problem. The concept of air assault capabilities emerged from the 11th Air Assault Division (Test) when it merged with 2nd Infantry Division. Eventually, the concept proved effective and the 1st Cavalry Division (Air Mobile) became the model for the future.

Hundreds of UH-1 Huey helicopters were deployed to Vietnam to support 1st Cavalry operations. In 1968, the Army designated the 101st as a new air mobile division. Over the following years in Vietnam, the 101st Airborne earned the nickname "Chicken Men" from the North Vietnamese, because of Screaming Eagle insignia. Reportedly, enemy commanders warned their units to avoid the "Chicken Men" because they were likely to lose any combat engagement with them. At the end of the Vietnam War, the 101st was the only division to stay active as air assault. It was also widely known as having so many aircraft assigned to the division that it alone was the seventh largest air force in the world.

Following Vietnam, the 101st was to recover as part of the new All Volunteer Force by recruiting new talent, modernizing its tanks, weapons, and helicopters, and training for major ground combat operations.

On August 2, 1990, Saddam Hussein of Iraq invaded Kuwait, compromising the country's national sovereignty and territorial integrity. The U.S. could not allow a flagrant violation of international law, especially against its allies and partners.

In operations *Desert Shield* and *Desert Storm*, the 101st got its first taste of Middle Eastern warfare. It had deployed, trained, and rehearsed for months in the Saudi desert to conduct offensive operations to repel Iraqi troops from Kuwait. This was the first time the division had been called upon since Vietnam and they were ready to flex their muscles. The division now had newly redesigned Apache attack helicopters that could conduct deep-penetration missions behind enemy lines and which consisted of an entire infantry brigade.

On January 17, 1991, at 0238, eight Apache helicopters from the 101st Aviation Regiment led by General Dick Cody, a future commanding general of the 101st, crossed into Iraq and fired the war's first shots, against radar sites near the border. The attack caught the Iraqi military completely off guard and paved the way for an opening from Kuwait to Baghdad for the large air and ground campaign. The new U.S. Air Force stealth bombers began pounding southern Iraq with massive ordnance strikes while the 101st and other ground forces massed on the border and waited for orders to begin their assaults against Iraqi troop locations and important infrastructure sites. The Screaming Eagles, along with other ground infantry and armored forces, were then ordered to commence offensive operations, cut off Iraqi supply routes to Kuwait and advance up the Euphrates River Valley south of Baghdad.

The 101st conducted the largest air assault operation in the world at the time. More than 60 UH-60 Black Hawks, 30 CH-47 Chinooks and numerous Cobra and Apache helicopters assaulted north, and past Iraqi positions. Reports show that many Iraqi units and soldiers, upon seeing such an overwhelming force, simply dropped their weapons and fled. The division earned another nickname, the "Lightning of Desert Storm" due to its speed and strike capabilities deep into Iraqi territory. The Strike Brigade carried on its legacy as a unit of the 101st Screaming Eagles and set conditions for follow-on forces.

CHAPTER 3

Training for War

In 2004, I met Captain Dan Morgan at Fort Campbell along with the other vets of the unit who had just returned after fighting in Mosul during the 2003 and 2004 invasion into Iraq. A large number of experienced soldiers had left the unit. They had been "stop-lossed" prior to the 2003 invasion and forced to extend their contract for the war. The Army had implemented the "stop loss, stop movement," program which required many veterans to deploy to combat. Now, in 2004 after the invasion, some of these guys were blasting out the door to go home and return to civilian life. New and inexperienced soldiers, such as me, were filling in the gaps.

Dan came from a military family and had been stationed all over the world. What made him different from other officers was that he came up from the ranks and didn't attend West Point. Although now a commissioned officer, Dan barely graduated high school. He played sports and got in fights. He spent a couple nights in jail "to calm down." He actually had to perform community service to get his high-school diploma. Like me, he committed to serve his country and enlisted as soon as he was old enough. Dan had found a passion where he could be in a team with a focus and mission. Promoted to captain, he commanded a company in another battalion during the Iraqi invasion. Soon afterward, the battalion commander, Lieutenant Colonel Rob Haycock, assigned him as his operations officer for the deployment and promoted him to major. He was a regular soldier at heart and we all respected him for it.

Young recruits like me were integrated into the unit, and we soaked up lessons these seasoned warriors shared from their experiences in combat and counterinsurgency operations. We ached for such experiences and were fired up for the chance to join the fight. I was assigned to 3rd Platoon, Alpha Company, 2-502nd Infantry Regiment as a rifleman/assaulter. It was the battalion's first day back on active duty. The mission was to refit the unit with lost or damaged equipment, get the men back to good health, refill the platoon with manpower, and start preparing for the next deployment to Iraq. Each light infantry company consisted of three rifle platoons and a headquarters platoon with the commander's group, communications, supply, the nuclear, biological, and chemical unit (NBC), fire support officer and forward observers (FSO/FOs), and a mortar attachment. Within a platoon, there were four squads each consisting of nine soldiers. One of the squads specialized in heavy weapons.

The new soldiers, referred to as "cherries," were bounced around the company and battalion areas and given direction to obtain equipment that we needed for both training and combat. During these details, I met Specialist Vosbein. He was in charge of the weapons maintenance and arms room. Vosbein was a very funny guy who always had the hugest dip of tobacco in his mouth I'd ever seen. I also met Specialist Byler. Byler was a mortarman attached to our company from the battalion's mortar platoon who had also been double-tapped to help in the supply room.

My squad leader, Staff Sergeant Girard, was the no-bullshit kind of non-commissioned officer you see in movies. He was very direct, to the point, and meant everything he said. As the senior squad leader in the platoon, he took NO SHIT from any other NCO or even officers for that matter. He knew his place, but he pushed the limits too. It was hell to be his soldier at first, but we learned quickly and everything he had us do was a learning experience. As tough as he was, he was protective of his soldiers, including us "cherries," which meant a lot to us. His leadership defined trust and discipline.

One time, another squad leader from a different platoon ordered us to do some kind of dirty detail. Girard unexpectedly stepped back inside and observed us doing this detail while the other squad leader's squad, all experienced combat veterans, just watched and smiled. Girard was pissed. We knew our place as well. We were new, but this was more of a jab at Girard because he and the other squad leader didn't get along. It had nothing to do with us. Girard immediately ordered us to stop and confronted the squad leader. They both started yelling back and forth inside the company hallway. Girard grabbed the other squad leader by his collar and drove him back into an equipment cage, which led to punches being thrown. Seeing the crowd that had gathered, the executive officer stepped up, quickly separated the two and handed them an ass chewing. It was clear to us at that point that we had a kick-ass squad leader who took no shit from anyone, especially when it involved his soldiers. It also painted a very clear picture that these men were still in a combative mindset and still on edge.

But Staff Sergeant Girard was not above having some fun as well. We didn't know it, but there was a "new guy" tradition about meeting the supply sergeant for the first time. Girard told another new soldier and me to go to the supply cage and ask for a PRC-E4. Pronounced as Prick! I knew from training that radios often start with PRC, meaning portable radio communication, such as PRC-77, an older radio version used in combat. E4 was an enlisted rank, known as Specialist in the Army. So, we assumed a PRC-E4 was some kind of new radio. We walked into the supply cage with our chests out and shoulders back, confident and ready to make an impression that we knew exactly what we needed when asking Byler for a PRC-E4. He was working behind the counter with another supply guy. I took a breath and said, "Excuse me Specialist, we were told to come here and request a PRC-E4."

"What the fuck did you just say!" Byler snapped back.

I didn't know what to say. Everyone there was trying not to bust out laughing.

Byler stood up to his full 6'3" and said: "You better get the fuck down and start beating your chest off the ground, you dumb motherfuckers!"

We stared straight ahead, not knowing what we had done wrong. Then, the whole place exploded in laughter. We immediately knew this was some kind of setup.

Byler jumped up on the counter and commenced with a five-minute smoke session of pushups, flutter kicks, and squats into an invisible chair until Girard told him to stop and said, "Okay, can we get some 100mph tape?" It was all done in fun and the spirit of unit camaraderie.

★

I thought basic training had prepared me for combat, but I was dead wrong. Major Morgan and our experienced leadership took us to the next level. "Your blisters will heal from digging a fighting position," Major Morgan would remind us. "There ain't no healing when you're dead." This was the mindset and became the norm in everything we did to prepare for combat.

The war experiences of our leaders were extraordinary, but what was most important was the ability to understand how those experiences defined the "why" of how we were training for our deployment.

Major Morgan described his deployment on the border of Iraq. The days went by in sweltering heat. Units conducted rehearsals, inventoried equipment, and loaded vehicles under the almost unbearable sun beating down on them. Every event was interrupted by air raid sirens and chemical battle drills that required gasmasks and bunkers. Everyone was in fear of an inaccurate, rudimentary Scud missile landing on them.

One evening Major Morgan remembers accounting for his soldiers between bunkers and looking up in the sky. He saw an explosion and thought that American air defense had successfully intercepted a Scud. In reality, a Patriot missile had hit a coalition aircraft that no one knew was in the area.

Eventually, the Strike Brigade consolidated in southern Baghdad to rest and refit as the U.S. Army determined future operations. Major Morgan, then a company commander, remembered a particular mission that provided a forewarning that this invasion was opening a bigger can of worms than they thought. He and a fellow company commander were given an operation to occupy key terrain back to the south. The brigade HQ directed Morgan's battalion commander to conduct a recon to occupy a linkup point in Mahmudiyah in order to pass through the 4th Infantry Tank and Mechanized Division.

Morgan took some elements of his unit and conducted a reconnaissance of the city as they entered south Baghdad. The city was littered with destroyed Iraqi tanks, infantry fighting and technical vehicles, also known as pickup trucks with mounted machine guns in the bed. The city was ablaze with burning vehicles and varying levels of destruction of buildings and homes.

Morgan maneuvered his forces into the city only to find his patrol surrounded by local Iraqis. Initially, everyone expected celebrations and gratitude from the local population. Not in this case. Morgan's vehicle, which was not armored, was surrounded by enemy fighters. "The stares between them and me were clearly telling me that we did not belong there. Their eyes seethed with hatred. Their silence was deafening. I thought we were going to have to fight to the death at any moment."

Throughout the recon patrol, Morgan did not place his M4 muzzle in view because the Iraqis were so close that they could reach in and grab the barrel. So, he had his 9mm in his left hand, pointing outwards at the local Iraqis. "I ran scenarios through my head that if our vehicle could not move anymore, I was going to empty my magazine into everyone's stomach around my door, get out, and empty every magazine in my M4 to either get my patrol moving again or die fighting. I had zero intention of being captured and decapitated."

Although the mission was successful, it resulted in 17 U.S. soldiers wounded in action. They encountered local Iraqis who threw grenades over walls and began firing weapons from multiple directions. Captain Wiley, the other commander, responded with massive firepower and won the battle. One of Morgan's medics, SPC Turner, shielded the wounded from enemy fire with his own body, earning himself a Silver Star.

Morgan said that this battle defined how the future fight would go in Iraq. It had the elements of sectarian violence and hatred of U.S. "invaders." The south was mostly Shi'a and anti-Saddam, while towns like this were hotbeds of Sunni extremism and pro-Saddam Baathist party members.

Soon thereafter, the Strike Brigade conducted another historic air assault in the northern Iraqi city of Mosul where it assumed operational control of the city and its government. The unit had shifted from offensive combat operations to stability and support operations in order to restore basic and essential services and create a stable and secure environment. Within a couple months, the Strike Brigade enabled elections in Mosul: the first free elections since the fall of Saddam.

Over the next nine months, the 502nd continued to provide security and services to Iraqi civilians. But success is always fleeting, especially in war. Major Morgan reminisced about how he and his platoon leaders and sergeants realized this was the case.

One day he was returning from a patrol as another patrol from his company was heading to a hospital to engage with a key local leader and hand out toys to young Iraqi children. As his convoy passed the other patrol, an IED consisting of 155mm artillery shells detonated on a lightly armored high-mobility multipurpose wheeled vehicle (HMMWV), or "Humvee," destroying the passenger side of the vehicle. It was a cargo vehicle that had soldiers in the back. The soldiers fell out of the cargo truck, staggering about the road and shooting wildly at the enemy.

Major Morgan's vehicle was on the opposite side of the cargo truck, but the explosion was strong enough that it ripped the canvas material off the driver's side door. Morgan's company first sergeant immediately set up a support-by-fire position. When Morgan got to the destroyed vehicle, he saw one of his platoon sergeants pinned among a heap of twisted metal. As he and the first sergeant pulled the metal apart to extract the sergeant, blood suddenly sprayed all over them. The metal from the radio mounts in the truck had been acting like a tourniquet on the sergeant's leg and now he was in danger of bleeding out. A combat medic who happened to be in the back of truck saw what had happened and immediately leapt over and placed a tourniquet on the wounded sergeant.

★

Today's battles are normally fought at the company and platoon levels, but this counterinsurgency was going to require decentralized leadership at the rifle team and squad levels. Companies and platoons bring heavy machine guns and mortars to bear against the enemy. However, based on counterinsurgency principles in winning the hearts and minds of a local populace, our success was going to be in our junior leadership's hands, and their small-unit tactics to work among the local communities and fight at a moment's notice. It was vital that we quickly learned to work together, to understand how to adapt U.S. Army doctrine to this new threat. We needed to understand call-to-fire missions with artillery, attack aviation, and fighter aircraft at the lowest levels.

These missions require a deeper understanding in coordinating air assets with ground units in order to identify and destroy the enemy, while preventing fratricide or civilian casualties. Combat communication usually resided with the platoon leader and his forward observer and radio telephone operator (RTO). Now, we had to learn them at the lowest level. Lieutenant Colonel Haycock demanded that Major Morgan and the company commanders had proficiency in everything down to the lowest level. The fact that we would be deployed in smaller teams required more training skills, and Haycock and Morgan knew that proficiency in skills would be critical in winning a combat engagement.

The privates, specialists, and corporals of the Iraqi invasion were now sergeants and staff sergeants, based on their success and the time in their previous ranks. The training got more realistic and intense as the months passed, based on our combat veterans' experiences from the last deployment. We started to grow together as a small unit and it could be seen in our tactics, discipline, candor, and cohesion. Tactics and techniques in our battle drills became second nature. We added complexity to the situations, such as civilians on the battlefield, suicide bombers, updated intelligence in route to an objective, and mass casualties. We began to operate well while responding fluidly to whatever the commander threw at us.

The training was chaotic and intense at times, but so was our downtime. On one particular evening I recall biting off more than I could chew. We had recently returned to the barracks after a long couple of training days in the field and had started our usual weekend routine of barbequing, drinking, and laughing about who knows what. On this particular night, I was hanging out with Sergeant Martin, Specialists Olsen and

Wharton and Private First Class Ketterling, and another buddy, Specialist Hernandez, who was from the mortar section.

After putting a little too many down, the conversation shifted to old traditions where a "cherry" got tied into a chair, damn near naked, and placed in the middle of the unit quad—the parade field—surrounded by the headquarters, barracks, and dining facilities. As the conversation continued into the night, I could see that something was going on and I was clearly not part of the conversation anymore. Battle buddies or not, I was not going to the center of the field naked without a fight. I told them that if they tried to put me out there, someone would lose an ear, eyeball, or pair of nuts.

Well, the alcohol took over and my ability to defend myself quickly disappeared. They made their move and the fight was on. Before I knew it, all six of us were tangling and fighting in the center of a barracks room. I found myself fighting and laughing at the same time while these jackasses tied me down into a chair. They stuffed my mouth with some dirty sock, carried me down three flights of stairs and then placed me into the middle of the parade field.

It was pitch black and there I was, all alone. It was quiet. I struggled to loosen the ropes, but I gave up, knowing that my teammates were sitting back in the dark, watching, drinking, and laughing. About 20 minutes later, the battalion staff duty officer walked by while conducting barrack checks and found me. He asked if I was okay. Of course, I couldn't respond with a sock in my mouth. He just laughed and walked away without another word. He left me there so he could go get other staff duty leaders to come see me. Yes, it was embarrassing, but all I could do was sit back and enjoy the rest of the night under the great Fort Campbell starlit night.

The parade field was home to many memories. It was a place where we welcomed in new command and staff and said farewell to others. It was a place where we'd nearly kill ourselves during combative training and push beyond our limits during workouts. It was also a place where some of the craziest parties I'd ever seen or heard of would occur. It was never unusual to see pockets of soldiers sitting around a fire near their barracks or by the parade field drinking some beers and relaxing. This area is where we bonded after long days and weeks of training.

One such evening led to a small group of 1st and 2nd Battalion soldiers getting into an alcohol-fueled argument about which battalion was better. We were young, full of piss and vinegar, and primed for a fight. Things got heated and a few of us started throwing punches. In a short amount of time, there were a couple dozen soldiers fighting in the middle of that great parade field.

The Military Police (MPs) arrived in force and began throwing gas canisters into the crowd to disperse us from what they thought was a riot versus a bunch of soldiers letting off steam. The MPs clearly thought they had things under control, but some of us ran back to our rooms, grabbed our issued gasmasks, and came back out to keep on fighting. Eventually, the alcohol and lack of oxygen from the gasmasks wore us down and before all was said and done, a half-dozen soldiers, give or take a couple, were detained.

What surprised me even more was that all of us involved, on both sides, were drinking beer together the next weekend and laughing about what had happened. I learned that was the way soldiers dealt with life. Fight hard, party hard, but always stay tight with the guys in your unit. We always had each other's back, on or off the battlefield.

★

In the fall of 2004, Alpha Company had a change of command. Captain Howard Donaldson took command of the company. The Ranger tab on his left shoulder proved he had the grit and experience to lead us, but his true character spoke to us more. Captain Donaldson was a smart, humble but driven leader. He commanded in a professional, stern manner, backed up by force of personality and sense of control and fairness. We had a running joke that since he looked like Denzel Washington, maybe he'd be tapped by Hollywood after he retired.

At about the same time, Sergeant First Class (SFC) Jonathan Tessar joined the company. Tessar would be Captain Donaldson's right-hand man serving as the first sergeant. I'll never forget seeing him on his first day in the unit. He had an old school, high-and-tight, flat-top haircut. His arms were tattooed from his wrists to his shoulders, and his uniform was covered with hard-won decorations. He possessed more tabs, schools and combat experience than I had ever seen on any other soldier in my early career. Including tabs for his service and schools in the Special Forces, Ranger School, and the 101st Airborne, his deployment stripes on his Class As ran all the way up his sleeve.

When I first met First Sergeant Tessar, I thought he was a smartass prick with a huge ego. He was extremely quick and would fire back at anyone who challenged his decisions or tried to get one up on him. We found that it was pretty much impossible to outwit or outdebate him on any military subject, especially tactics. As time passed, we viewed him as truly a good man and fine leader. Informed, educated, a straight shooter, he expected the same in return from his leaders and soldiers.

He began his career at the age of 17. He had wanted to be a soldier since the age of five and signed up as soon as he could. His first assignment was in Berlin, Germany, with the 5th Battalion, 502nd Infantry Regiment. He eventually transferred from Germany back to the United States where he came to Fort Campbell and joined 3rd Battalion (Widowmakers), 502nd Infantry Regiment. He then deployed on Operation *Desert Storm* with the Widowmakers and returned home where he eventually decided to become an Army Special Forces Green Beret, assigned to the 10th Special Forces Group in Germany. He also spent a lot of time in the Bosnian conflict.

After a career in Special Forces, he realized he missed the infantry. Special Forces is considered a special operation force that executes missions in small teams with minimal support in faraway places. He wanted to finish his career where it began—back with the infantry in the 502nd Infantry Regiment. His request was granted and found himself as the first sergeant of Alpha Company, 2-502, 101st Airborne. He wanted nothing more than to lead infantrymen on the battlefield and to share his expertise with a new generation of soldiers.

He was clearly well trained and a true believer in the counterinsurgency principles of winning the hearts and minds of the local populace. Nancy, his wife, was told by a local mayor in Bosnia that during his deployment there he would hand out lollipops to the local kids. When the kids saw him on patrol, or out helping the local Bosnian community, they'd always run to him and ask for candy. He was a great match for our company commander and we knew we were in good hands.

Captain Donaldson and First Sergeant Tessar formed the new command team tasked to prepare us for our next rendezvous with destiny. They infused their leadership philosophies in us, increasing tenfold our trust, grit, commitment, and overall combat effectiveness. What stood out to me more than anything else, was the fact that investing in their soldiers was priority number one. From Battalion leadership and down, they truly believed in making us better soldiers, fathers, and people in general. They wanted us to be lethal and successful on the battlefield, but also gentle and compassionate. It is a very difficult task to instill, but they did it. They were also very open to our opinions or suggestions, even at the lowest level. They may not have agreed with what we had to say, but generally speaking, we had a say in many operations, and that was huge. If we had a suggestion on a new piece of equipment that made sense, they'd say buy it. If we had input on an operation that seemed to be a great idea, or easier and safer manner, they'd say let's do it! It made us feel as if we had some ownership in the plan and the success of the unit. It was a Battalion-wide expectation. Leaders needed to be there for their men, and in the heat of battle, the men would be there for their leader. Thanks to their passion and experience, we were physically and mentally ready for combat.

In my opinion, we had the best company-level command team in the battalion. As leaders, they didn't make a big show wearing all their badges and awards. But the well-deserved tabs on their uniforms not only gave us confidence in their experience and leadership, but also set an example for us younger guys to work hard towards to achieving some of those same career milestones in the fight for country.

Our Battalion Command Sergeant Major (CSM) Pfrogner and Major Morgan had known each other for decades. They had served together as platoon leader and platoon sergeant. They were in the unit in Vicenza, Italy, and deployed to Bosnia together. They were part of the command team during the last deployment in Iraq, and now, back together for this one as well.

CSM Pfrogner was as tough as they come. During 12-mile ruck marches, he carried a folding stool with him along with his 50-pound ruck. When soldiers fell out, saying they couldn't finish, he would take out his stool and sit with the soldier and say, "Well, you ain't hurt, so let's sit here until you are ready. It is Thursday and I am going fishing Saturday so we have a couple days." He was ruthless on standards and grit.

We spent countless hours on the range learning how to shoot and move around vehicles. In between training iterations, NCOs would teach us the terminal ballistic effects of what occurred when our rounds struck the enemy and what their rounds did upon striking us and our gear, vehicles, and nearby structures. We trained weekly in advanced marksmanship skills and techniques that allowed us to shoot more accurately up close and further away.

One time, we accidently shot up a vehicle and we all worried that we were going to be in trouble. First Sergeant Tessar reported it to Major Morgan. He only asked if the truck could still be driven. We were a combat-focused battalion, he said, adding, "So what. As long as the equipment is functional, it doesn't matter."

We learned later why Major Morgan was not concerned about minor damage to equipment during training. During the invasion his unit had been engaged by enemy forces and had a vehicle and some equipment damaged. His element was falling behind the main assaulting force, so his soldiers grabbed sensitive items and key equipment; Morgan made a decision and used a thermite grenade to destroy the equipment so it would not fall into enemy hands.

A few weeks later, during a consolidation phase on the way to Baghdad, the previous brigade leadership called him into the Tactical Operations Center (TOC) tent and the brigade executive officer informed him that they were going to charge him for the damage. Morgan responded that he would not accept this and walked out of the command post (CP) because he had other priorities at the time, like combat and soldiers. His company was maneuvering aggressively from south to north into Baghdad and he was shocked that an administrative detail was hung up on destroyed non-sensitive equipment. The crucible of ground combat was paramount. He was mission-focused and the safety of his men was more important to him than non-mission essential equipment.

Our command team took the training regimen to a whole other level and beyond. It got so intense that guys were getting hurt falling off rappel ropes and while maneuvering through confidence course structures 20–40 feet high. Some were getting fractures due to running dozens of miles a week in kit on the roadways and during "river runs," where we'd literally run in and out of creek beds for miles. We'd run to the pools and swim until we'd about drown, then run back, and fight like hell with each other during brutal combative training days. We worked hard together, supporting each other beyond anything we had ever experienced in our civilian lives.

At one point, our company executed a live-fire training exercise in what was known as "a shoot house" on Fort Campbell grounds. A shoot house is a structure built for soldiers to train with live rounds in entering a building and clearing rooms occupied by enemy forces, otherwise known as close-quarter battle drills, or CQB. We learned how to move smoothly through indoor structures day or night, the importance of covering all angles, and advanced room-clearing techniques. Rather than just busting into rooms and attempting to dominate them by pure violence, we learned how to move with purpose, slow when you had to be and fast when you could safely do so. The techniques were eye-opening and proved much safer and more efficient than blasting through a room and exposing your unit, which could result in serious injury, or death, which in the end might lead to mission failure. First Sergeant Tessar's experience of combat and instructing Special Forces and other militaries around the world, were extremely beneficial in showing us how to use proven tactics that were safer and more effective than anything found in the conventional U.S. Army field manual.

Every experience during training had value. Like the time First Sergeant Tessar fired off a parachute flare during night exercises about 20 miles from base. It came down about 200–300 yards north of our site and set a large field on fire. The flickering flames spread quickly and grew so bright that the glow from the flames reflected off the clouds above. It was surreal. Our training exercise stopped as we considered options on how to stop it. We knew we had to call Lieutenant Colonel Haycock or Major Morgan, but we also tried innovative ways like digging trenches to prevent the fire from spreading across the fields and through the woods. Luckily, one of the area's frequent tropical-level storms blasted in and washed the fire out. It brought with it sustained winds of 60–75 mph; trees began falling everywhere, blocking our escape. We tried to take cover where we could but we were stuck outside, hiding under our vehicles from falling trees, hail, and lightning. Six to eight inches of water rushed past us as we laid on the ground with just our faces and upper portions of our bodies above the water. It got so bad that I literally started thinking a good chance existed that I was going to die in the woods of Fort Campbell training for war instead of fighting in it.

What makes the story memorable is the shared experience: not only did it highlight the unpredictability of circumstance in the field but highlighted our leaders' dedication to our safety. We were taking cover under vehicles while lightning was striking dangerously close, and here was First Sergeant, exposed, dodging lightning, hail, and debris to check on us. He rolled under the truck where I was sheltering with a few other guys. Seeing we were okay, he yelled: "You'll hardly ever remember the good times, but you'll never forget the horrible times. Enjoy the SUCK." He then rolled out from under the truck, got up and moved to the next location. Little did I know at the time how right he was. That single statement has stuck with me for almost two decades, and still stands true today.

The company leadership did not solely focus on mechanical battle drills such as shoot, move, and communicate training. We were also taught by RTOs, real communication experts in the 5th Special Forces Group, on how to use our janky communications at small-unit level. Some of us attended Arabic language training, while the rest of us focused on Iraqi culture, religion, and basic language phrases. We learned that we'd be fighting hardcore jihadi extremists who would be hell bent on breaking our morale by utilizing unconventional guerilla tactics. Our leadership aimed to help us understand everything we could about the enemy and their local culture so we could operate effectively in a counterinsurgency environment.

We were even provided an opportunity to do ride-alongs with Nashville police officers in order to try to pick up on how to read nonverbal indicators of persons in fear, under stress, or preparing to attack. There's no better source to learn this from than police officers themselves. Criminals always display signs of stress and anxiety. They also exhibit predatorial preattack cues, behaviors we needed to be looking for while patrolling the streets and fields in Iraq. This exercise developed into a training program that focused on our ability to detain insurgents, rather than engage with weapons, and gather much needed-intelligence for follow-on missions.

In the summer of 2005, we received orders that we would deploy to southwest Baghdad and take over an area of operations located in the northern Babil Province. The area became known as the "Triangle of Death" because it was a volatile Sunni–Shi'a fault line that encompassed 465 square miles. The region was a safe haven for AQI, and its proximity to Baghdad made it an attractive headquarters and support base for AQI operators attacking targets in and around the capital.

Our AO was mostly farmland, with sporadic villages and compounds, and intersecting canals. This terrain provided a defensive advantage to the enemy. Most of us, however, had no idea that it contained one of the most wanted terrorists in the world, Abu Musab al-Zarqawi and his army of battle-hardened jihadists.

CHAPTER 4

Deployment to Hell

In September 2005, Captain Donaldson and First Sergeant Tessar stood above us behind the company headquarters and explained the mission. It was our final formation at Fort Campbell before we departed for the airfield. They informed us that we had a tough fight ahead of us, but that we were ready. They stated our unit was expected to dislodge an unknown number of enemy fighters from strategic locations that they had controlled since the invasion. The enemy we were about to face consisted of entrenched Al-Qaeda elements, highly trained and financed Iraqi and foreign fighters who had specific bombmaking skills. These hardcore extremists facilitated the recruitment, logistics, financing, and bombmaking itself that built, deployed, and detonated VBIEDs against U.S. forces and Iraqi civilians with zero concern for loss of lives. They remained dedicated to a defensive jihad to create and instill fear, chaos, instability, and division between the Sunni and Shi'a populations in order to demonstrate that the U.S.-backed Iraqi government could not provide security and essential services to the population. AQI elements aggressively attacked U.S., coalition, and Iraqi forces in order to maintain freedom of movement and obviate the American public's support for the war. The attacks on the Iraqi government had sent shockwaves through their army and police forces, resulting in hundreds of Iraqi soldiers and police officers quitting in fear. Some Iraqi security forces who remained were committed to Iraq; however, a small percentage were playing both sides for financial gain or to kill Americans.

I vividly remember First Sergeant Tessar telling us to look to our left and right during that last formation, informing us that we'd be deploying to possibly the most violent and volatile region in Iraq. He said that some of us may get wounded, and some possibly killed. He reinforced how important it was that we remembered to take care of each other at all times, to watch each other's backs, to remember our training, and to never leave a fallen comrade behind. He paused for a moment, then said in his bellowing voice we all knew so well: "No matter what happens, you'll never be left alone, or left behind!"

Captain Donaldson finished his speech by informing us that the mission came first, but that he and First Sergeant Tessar would do their best to protect us and provide the best plans and equipment possible to ensure success on the battlefield. Last, he said they would be in the fight with us, every step of the way.

It was at this point that we realized we were about to step into a conflict against an enemy who hated us and wanted us dead. All the excitement from training had taken a backseat. The ranks were quiet, fixated on the words of our leaders. We had been watching the news and knew that our designated area was a major focal point. Despite our training and with all the combat stories we'd heard, we had no idea of what to truly expect, but we were ready to prove ourselves, to the enemy and each other. It was a formation and speech that many of us would never forget.

Shortly afterwards, we were released from formation to say goodbye to the families waiting nearby in an isolated area in the parking lot. Wives and their children, along with some mothers and fathers who'd flown in from around the country to see their soldier before he went off to war, were anxiously waiting to say their goodbyes. It was a hot day and the kids were running around like nothing was about to happen. They didn't understand where their daddy was headed, how long he would be gone, or what he was about to experience. Some would never see him again. Wives and girlfriends were in summer dresses. They knew and understood the seriousness of what was about to happen. Many wives had already experienced that horrible feeling before. It was almost like we were at a unit BBQ. Most veterans had no family there. They'd said goodbyes at the house and headed off to work.

I was single and had already said goodbye to my parents and family over the phone. I was ready to get the show on the road, but I knew it wasn't easy for those with families there and watched from afar as the mothers, wives, and children sent their sons, husbands, and fathers off to war. It was a sight that still sticks with me to this day.

As we made our way to the departure point, Major Morgan stood by the buses, kitted up in his combat gear alongside CSM Pfrogner. Suddenly, we heard the order: "Load up. Let's go!" All you could hear now were orders to move out. Reality was upon us.

We moved from our company headquarters to the airfield and loaded into a massive commercial airliner that flew us 16 hours to the hot desert of Kuwait. When we arrived, we loaded onto commercial buses. One soldier on each bus was given a full magazine to defend the bus and its two platoons of infantry grunts from any attack. It had got serious real fast. However, many of us joked about if we were attacked, we'd be fighting over the one gun to fight with!

During the ride, Major Morgan described his first bus trip to the Kuwaiti desert for the invasion. They had been on the same buses, but with no ammunition and could only travel at night, directed to close the curtains and keep their flashlights off. The bus interiors were lined with 1970s shag-like rugs with tassels dangling from the roof along with mini bells and ornaments. Morgan said it had felt like the TV show, Twilight Zone. At one point, he could tell they were no longer on the highway: "I peeled back one of the curtains on the side and saw all the other buses within a couple of feet of each other, jostling for the lead bus position. I was like, 'What the fuck, man!'" He said he couldn't help but think of the old movie *Ben Hur* and the chariot scene, except this time it was Kuwaiti Arabs and buses heading to war. He remarked how he had thought he was going to die in a flaming collision of buses and that would be his legacy. We all laughed. Soldiers have to have a unique sense of humor regarding death. It helps them cope.

Once we arrived at the staging area, our leaders updated us on the new tactics, techniques, and procedures that were being employed by terror groups in Iraq. Over the next two weeks we refined our battle skills. We got more training in searching for and finding explosive devices. We even did rollover and exit drills in helicopter and vehicle simulators. We confirmed our weapons systems for accuracy and functionality. We trained in the hottest part of the day to acclimatize to the weather and terrain and had to rearrange our kits. During this time, many of us also made sure things were in line with the man upstairs.

On a late starry night in September with a hot breeze, we loaded into Lockheed C-130 Hercules transport planes for the short trip to Baghdad International Airport (BIAP). The Air Force loadmasters informed us that BIAP was a hot zone due to enemy threats of shooting down American planes as they landed or took off. This meant that we would fly directly above BIAP and enter a tight downward spiral to avoid enemy fire. As we neared Baghdad, the aircraft started its spiral descent for a couple minutes, then landed hard, screeching to a halt. The aircraft ramp opened, and we were hit with the unique smell of Iraq, a country at war. It was a combination of burning diesel, feces, farm fields laden with livestock shit, and chemicals from firepits, a smell that stays with you forever.

While exiting the aircraft and waiting on the tarmac, mortar rounds struck the base to the northwest. Sirens went off across BIAP indicating an attack. The mortar rounds were nowhere close to us, but they confirmed that we were now in an active combat zone. We quickly learned that this was a common tactic by the insurgents, to bombard the airport with mortars or rockets while an aircraft landed in the hopes of damaging equipment or hitting U.S. personnel. We quickly shuffled off the asphalt towards a bunker, each of us carrying 100 pounds of gear.

Welcome to Iraq.

★

The next couple of weeks consisted of administrative tasks as the outgoing unit handed over their equipment and updated us on the combat situation. It was frustrating as hell. As Screaming Eagles, we wanted to take the fight to the enemy. However, we learned that before we did, we needed to inspect all the equipment and vehicles from the outgoing unit. We could not own the fight without owning the equipment. We met with our Army National Guard counterparts at every level from battalion commander to rifleman. These warriors appeared battered, tired, and clearly ready to get the hell out of the area and assume their new mission in Kuwait.

The most important part of this transition, known as "right seat–left seat rides," was the intelligence handover at the battalion and company level. The outgoing unit explained that they had attempted several times to push southwest to the Euphrates River in order to demonstrate presence in the area with hopes of squeezing enemy fighters out. The operation had resulted in complex enemy ambushes initiated by massive, deeply buried IEDs. Following the IED ambush, the enemy would lay down a heavy volume of fire, sometimes with mortars, from numerous angles to wound or kill as many soldiers as possible.

Visibly shaken from his experiences, the outgoing commander offered some sound tactical advice. He stressed that since we were the 101st Airborne, we needed to use our aviation assets to avoid the roads and only attack high-confidence targets of opportunity. However, our battalion had a different plan. Lieutenant Colonel Haycock and Major Morgan told him that we would use our air assets when needed, but we were going to fight up close and personal and own the ground. We aimed to meet the enemy on their turf and remove their freedom of movement, while building relations with the local populace. Unfortunately, the outgoing leadership had refused to conduct any operations past a certain boundary line. This strategy had allowed the enemy to create the safe haven known as the "Triangle of Death" from which they rained down unprecedented chaos and violence on Baghdad.

Our plan would require us to conduct a movement-to-contact operation into enemy territory, seize key terrain, and win over the local populace. Intelligence assets would inform our forward movement, while simultaneously identifying high-value targets (HVTs). It would be a complex counterinsurgency operation, consisting of fire and maneuver, stability operations, and kill or capture missions.

The biggest risk to our soldiers would be the movement down open asphalt and dirt roads. We needed to control the roads to prevent the enemy from moving fighters, supplies, money, and bombmaking materials. The outgoing unit had indicated a general area where they believed a lot of terrorists were active, so Lieutenant Colonel Haycock and Major Morgan planned to target those locations to take control of them.

Haycock did not dismiss the intelligence and recommendations of the outgoing unit. However, the battalion still had a mission and it could not be accomplished by doing the same thing for the next year. Counterinsurgency operations would be the primary means to win this fight, which would require us to live among the locals while hunting down the enemy. The main concern was that the battalion could not simply drive straight into the enemy stronghold because no one had a clear understanding of the people, enemy locations and activities, and terrain, meaning canals, roads, farmlands, and such like. Haycock wanted to probe the enemy safe haven from different directions to gain better situational understanding.

The thrust of the plan was to encircle the suspected enemy safe haven by maneuvering Charlie Company on the right flank to the west as a decoy. We needed to confirm enemy presence in the area and the degree of freedom of movement north of the suspected enemy safe haven in the Triangle of Death. Bravo Company would maneuver north of Charlie Company as a screening force to gain intelligence and provide early warning of enemy movement from the north into the enemy stronghold. Haycock and Morgan believed local population in the north was more amenable to our presence and would cooperate with us by providing information. Our third element, Headquarters, Headquarters Company (HHC), and Delta Company, would penetrate southwest down the center of our AO that was also considered safe for U.S. forces, with the purpose of establishing a battalion command and control tactical outpost codenamed Patrol Base Lion's Den. My unit, Alpha Company, would maneuver to the south on the left flank of HHC to locate the enemy and gain intelligence.

When operations commenced, the battalion hoped to deceive the enemy that we were attacking the enemy from east to west, so Alpha Company could maneuver slowly and deliberately north–south behind the enemy, eventually encircling their safe haven. Once the area was encircled and secure, we could then focus our intelligence assets, influence the local population, and destroy the enemy from within.

The previous unit was a mechanized infantry unit, so they mostly traveled in large armored vehicles, such as Bradley Fighting Vehicles (BFVs) and M1A1 Abrams tanks. Initially, these vehicles had been able to withstand IED attacks. However, the enemy then developed bigger and more sophisticated IEDs that rendered our best armored vehicles vulnerable. Casualties had mounted. Control of the AO deteriorated. Now, U.S. forces needed a different strategy.

First Sergeant Tessar and the other company leaders, along with Major Morgan and command leadership, had developed updated tactics based on new equipment and experience from the invasion. Morgan's previous unit had experienced multiple IED attacks and complex ambushes. We came up with a clearing strategy to travel down the roads more safely. The tactic was simple: get out of the vehicle and look for the bombs before they hit you. It sounded terrifying at first but it made sense. While we understood that we would be more exposed to IEDs, mortars, and gunfire while walking, it enabled us to spot an IED or its components before it exploded. This allowed us to either defuse or avoid them. As long as we were far enough apart from each other, we could isolate any one casualty and protect the rest of the convoy.

We would create a Vee formation that put the vehicles at the back of the Vee, while we spanned out looking for devices, detonation wires, triggermen, snipers, or other signs of enemy activity. We acknowledged the risk and would take turns volunteering to walk up front. We all wanted to serve and protect each other. Unfortunately, many of our soldiers were killed or wounded during such patrols. There was a phenomenal spirit in the Screaming Eagle. Sure, it could be frightening walking on point, but despite the threat, our courageous men would walk into potential danger every day to ensure the rest would survive. This speaks highly of our unit and what we were willing to sacrifice. The IED scout walking up front needed to focus on every detail both on and off the road. We accepted whatever fate God had in store for us.

The 120 degree Iraqi heat for a U.S. soldier carrying 30–50 pounds of ammunition, water, communication devices, signal jamming technology, a weapon and a Kevlar vest, was relentless. It never seemed to end. It seemed to get hotter as you maneuvered under the harsh sun, sapping the life out of you. The patrols were painstakingly slow and required multiple stops where we had to take a knee or lay down in the road to lower our profile, only to get back up again within seconds or minutes.

We developed an acute awareness of the IED signs such as disturbed dirt or fresh asphalt, wires, and local persons exhibiting suspicious and unique behavior. Once an IED was spotted, our Explosive Ordnance Disposal (EOD) experts would either disable it or blow it in place.

Most of the IEDs in early 2005 were command-wire detonated, meaning a triggerman was hiding nearby and waiting for us to travel into his kill zone before initiating the device. These IEDs could be buried underground or hidden on the side of the road, attached to a copper wire running from the IED to the triggerman. Our formation would help us find the wire, or even the triggerman at times, before anyone on the road entered the kill zone. Later, the enemy buried large bombs, including 500-pound aviation bombs, deep under the dirt or asphalt and used augers to drill even deeper to cover the detonation wires. These were hard to find and absolutely devastating to any military armored vehicle.

The IED search technique simply consisted of two soldiers walking off the road on either side and out in the fields in front of the trucks, approximately 50 meters or as the terrain permitted for observation and communication. Then, two more soldiers would walk in front of the trucks just off the road, behind the guys in the field. Sadly, despite our technique and constant adaptions, we would fail on occasions and many brave warriors suffered the ultimate sacrifice. It took extraordinary discipline in this heat and for 12-plus months.

The enemy counteraction to our formation would lead to cell phone- or radio-activated IEDs that were not exposed to the eye and much more difficult to locate. These became known as remote-controlled IEDs (RCIEDs). The enemy would conceal a small antenna or wire to protrude slightly out of the road or dirt in order to get a signal. This new device required us to walk closer to likely IED locations, substantially increasing the odds of losing legs or arms or being completely vaporized. There were plenty of occasions where one of us stepped on an antenna and froze, waiting for the split-second flash, loud boom, and then chaos. When it did not happen, the soldier was guaranteed to yell "FUCK!" that was always followed by relieved laughter and later a lot of pulling cotton back out of our ass cheeks because we were scared as shit at the time.

Some of the most lethal IEDs were victim-operated IEDs (VOIEDs) and house-borne IEDs (HBIEDs.) Since we were on foot and slowly taking over their terrain, the enemy smartly decided to place these IEDs where they believed we would patrol off the road, take routine breaks, meet with the locals, cross chokepoints, and even near or in homes or schools. Some were detonated when a soldier or truck touched a pressure plate buried just below the surface. Some used thermal and motion sensors that detonated when a soldier or vehicle interrupted the laser beam stretched across a road or an entrance to a building. These IEDs, sadly also led to many civilian casualties, including women and children. Sometimes the enemy would purposefully leave indicators of their presence, such as suspicious items or known AQI propaganda, in order to draw us into a building.

The mental stress in of itself with these daily operations was enough to make the common person crumble with fear and anxiety. We had no other choice. We were dedicated, trained, and confident, but we were tested every day. We could never allow the enemy to think he was striking fear in us. Courage and love for each other propelled us forward and into the face of our enemy. The bravery and mission mentality was an amazing sight to see.

AQI would surveil us daily from houses and markets, which required constant changes to our patrol times and routes. They were smart and were committed to killing us and bleeding us out, no matter how long it took them or how many of their own people were sacrificed. Their willingness to inflict death and destruction indiscriminately proved to be an advantage for them. It was difficult for us to wrap our heads around this kind of violence. It was a battle of grit, intelligence, and time.

Intelligence suggested that Abu Musab al-Zarqawi, the leader of AQI, and his unit of well-trained and -armed fighters, was using the southern area of our AO, known as Yusifiyah, to facilitate movement of fighters, spread terror, and plan future operations. Car bomb explosions in Baghdad were at an all-time high. The bombs were killing hundreds of innocent civilians every month and stopping them quickly became our number one task.

★

Our unit took full responsibility of the Yusifiyah region in early October 2005; it is located approximately five miles southwest of Baghdad,

20 miles south of Fallujah, and 40 miles southeast of Ramadi. Fallujah and Ramadi had been cesspools of insurgent activity where major battles had recently occurred between Sunni and Shi'a militias. Military operations had recently pushed many of the Sunni fighters, especially AQI, out of those regions and into the Triangle of Death. They used this area for future planning to destabilize Baghdad with an onslaught of VBIEDs, suicide attacks and relentless sectarian attacks. The Euphrates River and highways in this area served as major supply routes via farmlands, dirt roads, and canals that allowed the insurgents to infiltrate weapons and manpower into the cities, avoiding coalition checkpoints. While Haycock and Morgan reviewed the plan, studying the imagery with the company leadership, they remarked, "This is gonna suck. It is going to be a battle of ambushes. We need to drop in behind them … in their own fucking backyard."

Inside our AO was a nonfunctional Russian power plant that was clearly under the control of Al-Qaeda and which was a major staging area for enemy material and fighters. Morgan knew that in order to take away Al-Qaeda's freedom of movement we would need to take control of it. Because of its natural fortifications, he planned to subdue it first with a massive air assault into the plant itself and then take control from within. It was definitely a bold plan—to pinch AQI in the middle, disable their freedom of movement, and destroy their staging operations. Unfortunately, command headquarters was not part of the 101st Airborne and disallowed the operation. The 502nd Infantry Regiment had initially been assigned to 3rd Infantry Division and then to the 4th Infantry Division a few months later. They were a heavy unit and did not have an aviation arm with the requisite experience to execute an air assault at the time. Haycock and Morgan knew that a ground maneuver would lead to more casualties by having to take this heavily fortified power plant facility from the outside.

Our mission plan was to build patrol bases within the region in order to have a stable presence among the local population. By living close to the locals at multiple locations, we could gather crucial intelligence, build security and trust with local governance, and weaken the enemy from the inside. We hoped to have Iraqi security forces assigned to the area so we could transition responsibility for "winning hearts and minds" to the Iraqi government. Unfortunately, the Iraqi security forces would not venture into such a violent region after having their asses handed to them over and over again. We would be on our own in a wary and hostile community.

Fear of Zarqawi and his foreign fighters and their hatred of American infidels were deeply entrenched in the local population. The stifling Iraqi summer heat was second only to the searing hatred we saw in their eyes. Many of us newbies were shocked at how these people viewed Americans. Iraqi hatred penetrated your soul and burned through you. You knew a crosshair was on you everywhere you went.

Our patrols were to immediately probe into areas of the Triangle of Death that the National Guard unit had avoided over the past year. Mounted patrols consisted of three to four up-armored high-mobility multipurpose wheeled vehicles (UAHs), consisting of a driver, three seated soldiers who could dismount, patrol, fight, or make contact with the locals, and a gunner who manned a machine gun in the turret. Each patrol generally totaled nine to 12 dismounts. Companies would rotate their platoons in and out Forward Operating Base (FOB) Striker, located in the southern portion of BIAP, into the AO on a nonstop basis. The goal for our battalion was to build an overwhelming presence of troops, constantly pushing further into the AO to force the enemy to fight us. We needed to force combat so that we could occupy terrain owned by them and gather intelligence for future operations by collecting items from their bodies or extracting information from them if still alive.

The battalion headquarters, located on FOB Striker, would have intelligence, surveillance and reconnaissance (ISR) drones flying overhead, searching for possible IED activity, monitoring suspected VBIED factories, or collecting other types of intelligence on terrorist communication and activity. ISR was an extremely effective and relatively new technology that was growing at a rapid pace. The battalion layered so many ISR assets in gathering intelligence to observe enemy activity that manned and unmanned aircraft would constantly check in with us. All day and night we would hear chattering on the radios between the headquarters and ISR from the eyes and ears in the skies. This new technology was crucial to our future operations and mission to target and capture AQIZ and their foreign fighters.

CHAPTER 5

The Grim Reaper

The 31st day of October 2005 remains etched in the memories of our entire infantry brigade. We had just taken over the battalion AO two hours earlier. Company commanders, supply sergeants, and platoon leaders had accounted for millions of dollars of equipment from the outgoing National Guard unit. Sergeants had been running patrols with the outgoing leaders in order to learn the routes and key pieces of terrain, and details of the local Iraqi tribal leaders. Today, we owned the battlefield and had at least 12 months to go.

On this particular morning, the battalion intelligence section had received intelligence that the enemy had emplaced three IEDs along what was called "Route Motorhead," which had earned its name years prior to our arrival. No one really knows how it originated but we guessed it came from the rock band Motorhead. Motorhead ran north–south and dead-ended into an east–west canal that had a parallel dirt road. On the western side of the road were six other east–west roads that were pretty evenly spaced out down the length of the road.

On the eastern side of Motorhead, a north–south canal prevented our vehicles' freedom of movement to the east. The terrain provided excellent positional advantage to the enemy. They could hit our patrols from the east, then escape on foot into the canal where our vehicles could not pursue them. The northern portion of the road was fairly straight, which gave the enemy multiple vantage points for early warning to their IED cells upon seeing U.S. forces enter the battlespace. The southern portion of the road had plenty of S curves, which created dead space, or blind spots, for them to attack us in excellent kill zones. We were blind until we came around the curve. This route was full of craters from previous IED explosions. The only way to maneuver down this road was either on foot or pushing the vehicles at high speed to swerve around the holes like an Olympic slalom skier.

The farmland terrain around Route Motorhead was flat and you could see for miles by just getting up on top of a gun truck. The farms were compartmentalized by irrigation canals that were hidden by high reeds and brush along the sides. This compartmentalization made it difficult to patrol on foot or pursue the enemy. Most canals had crossing points, ideal for pressure-plate explosives aimed at our foot patrols.

Houses were sparse and so was the local population. We rarely saw people, which we initially attributed to their fear of us. We soon came to realize that many of them had left the area because they had seen the fight coming and wanted to be out of harm's way.

According to Major Morgan, the intelligence on the IEDs to go look for was reliable. We had 10-digit grid coordinates, which meant that the IEDs were within one meter of the location on the map, and on Route Motorhead. The battalion wanted us to confirm the location because our signal and human intelligence analysis indicated that this route was likely the main facilitation route for AQI and Zarqawi's foreign fighters. If we could confirm this intelligence, we could clear the route and begin controlling an avenue of approach towards Zarqawi.

At around 0400 hours, First Sergeant Tessar walked into the company CP on FOB Striker and told me I was not going on today's patrol. Then he directed me to go wake up SPC Byler. I was pissed off. The day prior I had been told I would be going out on this patrol. I had not as yet left the wire, meaning the FOB, and was very excited to be getting out onto the battlefield. I pushed back on Tessar's call, but he quickly shut me down: "Get Byler!"

Byler and I were extremely close. We had damn near become brothers after the past year of training and living together in the barracks and off post. Byler was a proud Texan from Ballinger. He never shut up about how awesome Texas was and how everything there was bigger and better. That was Justin Byler. He and another close friend of mine, SPC Hurst, from Alabama, often got into it over who was more "Southern" and had the better football teams.

I treasured our bond and would find myself sitting back and smiling, enjoying hearing them argue. I would always slip in comments to fuel their fiery debates; they cracked up once they realized I was fucking with them. These guys were extremely smart, both had Type-A personalities, and would sacrifice themselves for each other at the drop of a hat.

Byler was the exact kind of guy I wanted on my side when the shit hit the fan. Whether it was a fight in a bar or on the battlefield, one thing was for sure, Byler would be right there beside you ready to fight when things went sideways. His loyalty to missions and friends was second to none. In everything he did, you didn't just get a slice of the Byler pie, you got you the whole damn thing.

Byler was the first cot on the right only about five steps in from the tent flap. I walked in and sat down at the end of his cot. I opened his trunk where he always kept awesome snacks and ripped one open. Half asleep, he rolled over slowly and wanted to know what was going on. Sitting in the pitch black, I told him that First Sergeant had taken me off patrol and he had to go. He slowly sat up in his bed, wearing only underwear, grabbed his hygiene kit, and slipped on his sandals.

We walked and talked quietly under the night sky on the way to the latrines. We continued talking for a few more minutes back in the tent while he was getting his gear ready. He told me he had a bad feeling about this patrol. I wish I had paid more attention to this conversation. I was a "cherry" and too busy stealing his snacks since I hadn't eaten for most of the night. I learned that every conversation with your fellow soldiers prior to a combat patrol had to be treasured because you just never knew what was next.

As he walked out the door, he turned to me and said quietly, being careful not to wake anyone up, "Hey, if I don't come back, be sure to tell them to bury me in my sandals and underwear 'cause where I'll be headed it will be hot!" I told him to shut the fuck up but called dibs on his treasure trove of treats in the trunk if he didn't return.

He lumbered out of the tent into the starlit night with a chuckle and his huge Texas smile. That was Byler, always breaking the ice with a joke.

Looking back, I feel like I should've known, but I was too inexperienced at the time. Why did Byler make that comment? Was it just the sarcastic humor that warriors have in combat to deal with the impending threat of death? I'll never know or understand, but when I think about that morning before sunrise, I wonder if there may have been some kind of spiritual presence somehow giving me a sense of Byler's fate.

★

First Sergeant Tessar and the patrol leader, Sergeant First Class (SFC) Geleney, the acting platoon sergeant of 2nd Platoon, gathered the patrol together and prepared to push down Route Motorhead to confirm the location of the IEDs. The UAHs were staged and ready. NCOs conducted pre-combat inspections of their soldiers, weapons, ammunition, and equipment. It was the first push south down the long north–south route into no man's land.

Nerves and tensions were high knowing that massive IEDs were buried in the road with triggermen on constant watch, waiting to attack passing patrols. Enemy contact was guaranteed that far south. The patrol assembled around the lead truck and discussed the plan.

Then SFC Geleney yelled, "Lock and load!"

Fully kitted warriors climbed into their trucks at pre-dawn, to meet the enemy in what would probably be our company's first fight against AQI.

Sergeant Tessar was overwatching the patrol from the second truck from the front. This is normally where the senior leader could best control the formation. He wanted to go along with the first few patrols to give confidence to his soldiers and ensure that his junior leaders gained experience the best way possible. Byler was Tessar's driver. PFC David Martin manned the gun up top in the turret, while PFC Adam Johnson was riding in the rear to be used as a dismount/assaulter.

The UAHs were fully enclosed with heavy armor on the sides, rear, and front. Based on the increasing IED attacks since the invasion, our UAHs had bulletproof glass and reactive armor on the doors, designed to minimize the effect of rocket-propelled grenade (RPG) attacks. However, the bottom of the vehicle was the weak point: it was flat and unarmored.

The enemy knew that. The majority of the blasts were increasingly from beneath the vehicles. The flat surface of the UAH bottom simply absorbed the blast, along with the occupants. Once the patrol passed over Route Tampa and started down Route Motorhead, they assumed the Vee formation to look for IEDs.

2nd Platoon soldiers had been walking on and through the fields, canals, and roads for hours. They had found two of three IEDs. The Vee formation and discipline was paying off. The heat was stifling and challenging everyone's stamina. It was so hot that mirages appeared in the distance. After defusing both IEDs, they debated mounting up in the vehicles and moving forward a few hundred meters versus walking in formation. The success of the patrol in finding the bombs using the accuracy of the intel, coupled with the heat, resulted in the platoon deciding to mount up and drive to the final location.

What they didn't know at the time was that there was a communication dead zone in the area. No one knew this because no one had been this deep into AQI enemy territory. Second, AQI fighters had been patiently watching them the entire time, waiting for the right time and place to strike.

The patrol jumped back into their trucks and followed First Sergeant Tessar who picked up speed and maneuvered around the front truck to take the lead position. Byler drove around the front truck to guide the patrol towards the next targeted IED location. Private Martin, the gunner, observed enemy personnel a short time later and began engaging the fighters in a canal. Byler slowed the truck to help Martin with accuracy, when suddenly, their truck was struck underneath by a massive IED.

Everything to the front disappeared in a violent volcanic-like eruption of dirt and asphalt. The blast was so powerful that it bent the UAH in half, lighting it on fire and throwing it into the air as if the rules of gravity did not exist. The explosion ripped open the doors and immediately ejected SPC Byler into a nearby reed line on the driver's side of the truck. Private Martin was thrown into a nearby field on the passenger side of the truck. Both Byler and Martin were killed instantly. First Sergeant Tessar and Johnson sustained major trauma with life-threatening injuries.

The vehicle was burning so hot that ammunition and explosives inside the truck started exploding, sending pieces of metal and ammunition in all directions.

SFC Geleney immediately took control of the patrol and set up a defensive posture. He maneuvered to each gun truck, checked on his men, and gave them sectors of fire to engage the enemy. They were now in a 360-degree firefight. Geleney and his other NCOs, Staff Sergeant Thomas, Staff Sergeant Maloney, Sergeant Allen and SPC Hammer, without hesitation bailed out of their vehicles into the barrage of incoming rounds, returning fire, as they selflessly raced towards the wreckage in order to save any survivors. Unfortunately, it got worse. The enemy began firing mortars onto their position in addition to the heavy machine-gun fire.

Firefights in combat movies seem to last an eternity. It is so far from the truth: firefights normally only lasted a few minutes, or even seconds, in Iraq, but they were violent.

Geleney and his warriors were in a state of shock. No IEDs had been this huge. The explosion created a crater easily six feet deep and six feet wide. It is hard for most people to understand, but once warriors recognize the likely fate of death in combat, they can operate with clarity of mind, selfless service for each other, and courage in action. Soldiers, especially combat infantry grunts, sign up to fight in battle, knowing the risks. On this day, these brave men were taking the fight to the enemy, aggressively and courageously until they were hit by the IED. First Sergeant Tessar and three amazing warriors were gone in a blink of an eye.

The enemy attack shook the battalion. Outside of a couple officers and sergeants, no one had any combat experience. The battalion TOC on FOB Striker did not know how to process Geleney's information flow over the radio. Soldiers and young officers were screaming, "What do we do? What the fuck happened? Who was killed?" Discipline was lost, which did not help the soldiers on the ground under attack, who were trying to fight, and control the chaos under fire, with KIAs all around them.

Fortunately, Sergeant Major Crabtree, Morgan's operations sergeant major, and Major Morgan came into the TOC and took over the radios.

Morgan directed SFC Hunter, the TOC NCO-in-Charge (NCOIC) to gather up the staff officers so they could manage information flow. Morgan learned that there were four KIAs, that the patrol had stopped receiving effective fire and was able to establish security around the blast site. He took over radio control with Geleney on the ground and calmed everyone in the TOC.

Morgan and Crabtree immediately requested direct support from attack aviation in order to extend Geleney's eyes and ears on the ground. Second, Haycock was kitted up in minutes and hauling ass to the patrol with a ground quick reaction force (QRF). Eventually, the firefight ended soon after the Apache helicopters were on the scene and Geleney could start the difficult task of cleaning up the battlefield of our fallen heroes and equipment.

Tessar and Johnson were extracted from the vehicle but had already succumbed to the explosion's devastating effects. Martin was located next and Byler was found last. It took hours to search and locate their remains. All four soldiers were taken from the scene by Eagle Dustoff, an aerial medical evacuation (medevac) team, and reported as killed in action.

Protocol required an after-action review (AAR) as soon as possible after the incident. This AAR determined that the patrol's Blue Force Tracker (BFT), a computer-generated map linked to Global Positioning Satellites (GPS) to identify a unit's vehicle location on the ground, was lagging by approximately 800 meters due to a temporary communication dead space. This meant that Tessar's vehicle was actually over the massive IED they were looking for, not 800 meters east, or short, of the IED like they thought. The satellites' capability to track their vehicle on the map in their truck lagged behind the actual location.

We were not fighting a 9-to-5 war. Haycock and Morgan immediately seized on the mantra that "we are not going to drive to work every day." From now on, all patrols packed two to three days' worth of operational supplies in order to maintain pressure on the enemy and establish a sustained physical presence among the local population instead of rushing back to base after the operation was completed. To address the issue of communication dead spaces, the intelligence and communications sections created a map of dead zones, which allowed us to plan for relay stations during operations. We were learning … and fast.

The battalion HQ required us to not only conduct the medical evacuation, but account for and retrieve all U.S. salvageable equipment off the battlefield to make sure that the enemy did not gain any intelligence or special equipment. Major Morgan stated: "We are not leaving anything or anyone on the ground that gives the enemy a sense of victory. All that people will see is that someone blew a hole in the local population's road." We remained on site until we had cleared the battlefield. It was hard to do, but it was the right thing to do.

The task at hand, however, did not take away any thoughts, memories, anger, hurt or emotions. We were shocked over the power and violence of the explosion. What we did not say to each other was the thought that any one of us could be next. Among the debris, we found Byler's rifle, but not his personally purchased M4 carbine rifle bipods. This tore at my soul because I felt that we'd left a piece of his identity on the battlefield. I felt like I had failed him. Months later one of our patrols stumbled across the bipods in the middle of a nearby field once the foliage had died back. I kept them and years later I mailed them to Byler's brother in Texas, as a keepsake from his heroic brother.

The battalion directed Delta Company, commanded by Captain Crain—a compassionate, witty, tactical genius—to assume control over our AO for a few days. The battalion commander wanted our company to grieve and formally memorialize our fallen heroes. A couple days went by then we buried our emotions and got back to work.

For us "cherries," right out of high school, we wanted glory and excitement. Tragically, we learned on day one that killing or being killed is the true nature of war. We had trained and rehearsed for this, had discussed the morality of killing, but we never truly reflected on being killed and how to balance the psychological contrast between the three: kill or be killed or not to kill. After that fateful attack, reality hit hard.

Devotion to mission and the bonds we shared would drive us to fight the enemy to the death and allow us to accept our fate. Death in combat has to be expected and the loss of our company first sergeant and friends fueled our passion to take the fight to the enemy. We were now stoked by duty and vengeance. The fire in our souls was burning bright and hot.

I walked out of my tent into the night the evening after we lost our guys. I remember looking up at the sky and all the stars. Iraq has no ambient light so the stars light up like they are on fire. There were millions of them. I could not grasp the irony of war that after so much violence, nature and life continued with such beauty. It made no sense. I sat down on a concrete barrier and reflected about what Tessar had told me a couple days before the fateful patrol. We were walking back to our tent in the cold, dark October night. I saw Tessar's warm breath meeting the cold, brisk air. He looked up at the stars, seemingly speaking to himself, and said that he had a really bad feeling about this deployment and wanted to get right with God. He looked at me and said, "That sixth sense … it's almost always right. Pay attention to it."

My mind drifted to Byler's sarcastic comment that if he died in combat, I needed to make sure they buried him in sandals and underwear. I laughed quietly and dropped my head onto my chest, remembering how Byler had lived and how I needed to celebrate his life. Suddenly, an overwhelming feeling of despair overcame me. Family popped into my mind. I was deeply disturbed knowing that all four families back in the States were about to receive the worst news of their lives. Something did not seem fair that they would learn of their deaths from someone other than us. We were his team, his brothers, his family away from home. Yet, we would not deliver the news or grieve with the families. The Army would send uniformed soldiers. As a matter of fact, the battalion shut down all communication back to the States for a few days to prevent anyone from saying anything that might get back to the family until they could be officially notified.

CHAPTER 6

Kill Zone

On the morning of November 12, 2005, a section of 3rd Platoon, Alpha Company, was tasked to conduct surveillance on another portion of Route Motorhead to eventually establish a forward patrol base in the area. Our battalion had been hard at work pressing AQI and gathering more intelligence on their network.

New technology, such as signals intelligence, counter-IED electronic systems, and drones, increasingly enabled our offensive capability to find and destroy the enemy. We would use any means to force AQI fighters to get on their radios and cell phones. Once they began chatting, we would learn more about their plans and movements. A lot of the time we would simply go on patrols to force them to engage us. Intelligence units would then monitor their radio communications, and based on their radio chatter, ambush attacks by both ground fighters and IEDs, and other intelligence efforts, we started creating a template of the enemy.

We would conduct multiple surveillance overwatch positions to expose likely IED ambush sites on Motorhead, and as time passed, we would push deeper into AQI territory. We needed to conduct a reconnaissance-in-force and develop freedom of movement for our logistical lines of communication. To do this, the battalion decided to execute a penetration operation down Motorhead, sequentially clearing the road and 1,000 meters on either side of the road. We would push south clearing and occupying key terrain and establish a patrol base that would be our base of operations for the next year.

We loaded up four Humvees and headed out just after sunset, utilizing the darkness to conceal our movements. Our patrol consisted of 20 warriors in four heavily armed gun trucks.

As per the standard procedure, we would run completely blacked out, meaning absolutely no white lights were allowed. We used powerful infrared lighting systems and night vision devices to safely navigate with and identify potential IED triggering devices on the road. This limited visibility technique helped prevent AQI fighters from observing and alerting others as to our location. Unfortunately, the loud diesel engine could never be suppressed. If AQI fighters were within half a mile of us when we entered the AO, they'd hear us coming.

In order to maintain surprise at night, we would locate a house, clear it and hide our vehicles behind the back, setting up a command control position as we patrolled the area. The owners of the house were then ordered to give us their phones and told to go to sleep. Soldiers would watch over them to ensure that was exactly what they did. We would always extend our gratitude and respect to them for "allowing" us to use their structure for our purpose. Sometimes we'd give them cash. Other times, they'd refuse it and just stare at us with hate. Either way, we did what was necessary for the safety of the men and success of the mission.

The local population stayed in at night. Anyone on the road after midnight received a lot of attention from us. The rules of engagement at the time allowed us to define hostile intent or a hostile act. For example, if you were digging alongside the road, or even carrying a shovel at night, you met the criteria of hostile intent and could be killed. Sometimes, however, it could be a problem. During the summer, farmers dig at night because it is too hot in the day. We had to make judgement calls and, sadly, we made mistakes.

That night the wind was blowing but the sky was clear. Staff Sergeant Crispen was leading the patrol. Everyone was focused. We took over a house and set up surveillance. About halfway through the night, Corporal Zamora observed a subject walking towards the road from an open field to the west. He had what appeared to be a shovel in his hands. We passed the information up by radio to company and battalion headquarters. The preferred method would have been to allow him to dig, let him leave the location, and call in air assets to follow his movements from the air. Then, we could develop the intel picture for future operations. However, HQ informed us that there were no air assets in the area that night. Without air assets, it was up to us to either to kill or capture him to avoid him alerting any terror cell nearby. We also wanted to gather intelligence from the items he might have been carrying.

Corporal Zamora was the designated marksman and carried an enhanced M-14 carbine. After further deliberations with our higher headquarters, he carefully acquired his target using night vision to gather a good sight picture through his scope and fired one round from about 300 yards out. The rifle fired a heavy 7.62x51mm round that was ideal for long-range engagements, but it also had a tendency to strike a target and pass through it since it was a non-expanding cartridge. A good head, spinal, heart, or pelvis girdle strike would drop a fighter, but anywhere else could lead to the bullet traveling right through the body. The man immediately bent over and dropped his shovel. He then took off running to the west, where he quickly disappeared into the nearby foliage of the canal. Apparently, Zamora had missed his target, or the bullet had passed right through him. Being a country boy at heart, I had seen this happen numerous times while hunting deer. I knew that the shot could still have hit him, but the only way to confirm this was to go look for him and see if there was a blood trail.

The loud unsuppressed shot from the M-14 had rung out through the rural night. The enemy was used to hearing random gunshots, so Zamora's single crack in the middle of the night was not too much of a concern. We knew it could be game time and started taking defensive positions in and around the house. We were itching for a fight with AQI. Then Staff Sergeant Crispen gave us a quick patrol order and contingency plan and we moved out quietly under night vision goggles to search for the man/fighter. Unfortunately, he was long gone. All we found was his shovel. We dared not turn on white-light flashlights to look for blood. That would immediately give away our location, so we were unsure if it was a good hit or not.

The sun rose and the heat began to sear into our equipment and skin. We loaded up into the vehicles and began pushing methodically south down Motorhead. We wanted to get to the objective, the southern end, and look for a potential patrol base, but we had to be patient. We did not want a repeat of the catastrophic IED blast of the month before. Tensions were running high. Sweat was pouring down our flushed, exhausted faces.

Sergeant Crispin got out with PFC Hursey, and a couple other dismounts, to start clearing the route ahead. We were anticipating an attack after firing on the man with the shovel only hours earlier. We had to assume they were waiting for us. On this particular day, my squad was mounted up in the vehicles to watch over the dismounted patrol. I had rear security and was positioned in the turret with an M-2 .50-caliber heavy machine gun.

Sergeant Crispin and PFC Hursey identified a previous IED site that had been filled in with fresh asphalt. Normally, an IED blast would be filled with concrete by locals under the supervision of our military engineers, who would then mark them with a sequence of letters and numbers. Our platoon leader, Lieutenant Worley, got on the radio and asked battalion command if the unmarked hole had been filled recently. Battalion relayed back to us that it was unknown.

We had to make a choice: we could either halt movement and isolate the area for an EOD team or push past the suspicious location and mark the map for a follow-up route-clearance mission. We chose to chance it because we were impatient and didn't want to wait for EOD. Each truck carefully circumvented the blast hole, one truck at a time, and drove around it and stopped south of the crater in order to continue searching for secondary IED threats. We had a couple dismounts on the road so we had to wait for them to continue clearing ahead of us.

While we maneuvered the trucks into a standard security posture—a herringbone formation facing outwards and staggered on the left and right of the road facing south—Staff Sergeant Crispin and his small team were just off the road speaking with an Iraqi woman in her front yard outside a nearby house. She was wearing full Arab dress and was shaking her head and waving her hands just above her head, indicating that she did not know anything, while asking them to leave her alone. But she had to know something because the hole was basically right in front of her house. She was adamant that she had not seen anyone. Locals always claimed there were no bad guys around, even after a full-on firefight in their front yard. If they did confirm local fighters were nearby, AQI would kill them and their entire family, so they had to play dumb.

Suddenly, a massive explosion rocked the thick, humid air. As the concussive shockwave coursed through the air like a tidal wave, it shook our bodies from what felt like the inside out. The explosion sent manhole-sized pieces of jagged 12-inch slabs of hardened pavement hundreds of feet into the air. A huge cloud of dust billowed outward hundreds of yards off the road towards Crispin and the Iraqi woman, obscuring them, his team and the truck in front of me with PFC Packer and SPC Knight. The hole left in the roadway was so large that we could no longer back out or even turn around. The enemy had deliberately cut the road in half. Once again, we were boxed in.

Approximately 100 yards remained to the end of Motorhead, which had a dirt road going off to the right. Immediately to the left was a large canal. On our right, a deep ditch with trees prevented us from maneuvering off the road and through the field. We were in a perfectly designed kill zone.

No one could see each other. Leaders were screaming through the cloud trying to account for their soldiers: "Sound off!" and "Don't move! Get down!" After a few minutes, the dust began to settle, allowing us to consolidate and reorganize. The rear two trucks had been consumed by dust and debris. However, fortune was on our side and no one had been wounded or killed.

We were in a really bad spot and had to react fast. In any ambush, the immediate reaction is to return fire and assault the enemy; however, no enemy was shooting at us. Since we had no casualties, we could have driven forward and gotten the hell out of the kill zone, but we'd risk a more complex IED ambush and a potential for enemy mortars and machine-gun fire. We chose to stay where we were and expand our security zone.

Sergeant Crispin's team found additional command wires that led towards the road in front of lead truck, and farther south. Thank God we had not driven forward. Crispin and PFC Ayala broke off from the main element and immediately began pulling wires up off the ground and cutting them. This was a dangerous move and normally not recommended, but they made the decision to take the risk to protect all of us while completely exposing themselves to potential enemy fire.

The team rapidly traced the wires back to the trigger point in a nearby reed line. They split up into smaller teams. One team found a red blanket in a hide among the reeds. On top of the blanket was a cup of chai tea that was still hot. There were over a dozen separate triggers to different IEDs along the road. Later, Major Morgan asked for a schematic for an AAR and when he saw this particular site, he said it looked like a "spaghetti bowl of command wire to IEDs." This fighter, and most likely others, had simply been sipping tea waiting to attack us.

As Crispin was exploring this triggerman's site, the mounted gunners identified numerous small groups of enemy fighters running through a building complex southwest of our location. They were moving fast, wearing the typical AQI garb of Adidas-type jogging pants, balaclavas, and load-bearing vests. They started taking rooftop positions to gain observation and elevated firing advantage.

Lieutenant Worley attempted to report the situation to battalion command because we did not have enough combat power to maneuver on to the enemy locations as the enemy had us trapped with an IED strike. We needed attack helicopters or UAVs to gain advantage. The terrain of canals and reeds obscured and prevented our gun trucks from being able to provide effective fire against the enemy locations. However, the lieutenant couldn't get through. We were in another unidentified communications dead zone. We had to rely on text message over Blue Force Trackers (BFT), which also provided global positioning through satellites, but it was slow.

Major Morgan got the text and contacted an AH-64 Apache unit, call sign Viper, and sent them our way. In addition, Lieutenant Colonel Haycock mobilized his ground QRF but we knew it could take upwards of an hour to reach us. The Viper element arrived on scene and began looking for the fighters who knew to hide. The aviation element of two Apache AH-64 helicopters with electro-optical and infrared capability for observation as well as Hellfire missiles and 30mm machine guns were on station for 15 minutes but were too low on fuel to remain and headed back to base. Fortunately, Major Morgan had sent a Shadow drone to support the battalion commander QRF movement to the area, so we were able to reorient the drone to locate enemy fighters and direct movement on the battlefield once the Viper element left.

Meanwhile, Sergeant Crispin's dismounted patrol made it to the intersection of Motorhead and "Fatboy," the dirt road that ran west, in order to attack the AQI fighters hiding among the buildings. The small team cleared a structure and Crispin deployed designated marksman Corporal Zamora and a few others to a nearby rooftop to cover his movement, and employ precision fire. He reported that fighters with weapons had got into three white Bongo pickup trucks and quickly fled the area west on Fatboy.

The team reported this information to me as the RTO back at the trucks, and I relayed the information to the Vipers that were back on station with full tanks. One Viper identified the enemy vehicles and engaged the front truck with rockets, destroying it and forcing the other two behind it to stop. The fighters in the other two trucks immediately bailed out and ran into the nearby reed lines and palm groves, effectively concealing them from Viper's sights and thermal imagery.

Then, all hell broke loose.

A large number of fighters had apparently stayed behind to provide cover while the AQI fighters in the pickups attempted to flee the area. In the midst of the barrage of small-arms fire, we started hearing distinct cracks and thumps. The enemy had a sniper and a mortar team shooting at us. We were fighting the largest group of AQI fighters that we had so far encountered. We were surrounded.

Private Trofatter, Private Ayala, and PFC Gordon were engaging the enemy from a rooftop and giving out target locations when an HBIED detonated underneath the stairwell of the house. They suddenly disappeared amidst the dust and debris of the explosion as the building collapsed, but they had dropped off the side of the structure. Luckily, they had sustained only minor bruises, cuts and temporary hearing loss. Fortunately, the only portion of the roof still intact happened to be the portion where they had been. Talk about crazy luck. That was war. You never knew what would happen.

Lieutenant Worley and his team sprinted across an open field to the destroyed house and joined the erstwhile rooftop team to set up a defensive posture. Then he ran back to our location so he could update the battalion HQ. I watched him running north up Motorhead to our gun trucks. When he got to the first gun truck, he slowed down to catch his breath. As he passed the third truck, another massive IED detonated directly beside him. The IED had been buried deep in the middle of the road. In the earlier chaos and confusion we had missed the command wires on that side of the road. This massive blast severed the road again, separating the rear truck from the other three. Worley disappeared in the storm of dust that enveloped the site.

The concussion of the blast rocked trucks three and four and knocked both PFC Packer and me backwards into our gun turrets. I remember seeing in slow motion pieces of asphalt easily three to five feet wide, pass over our vehicle. I pulled myself back up into the turret and began looking for Worley. The only thing I could see was dust. The worst part of an IED attack is anticipating the sight of the destruction of your comrades after the dust has settled. It tears you up inside.

Our combat medic was sitting in the front passenger seat. I ducked down and yelled, "Find Worley!" He was still in shock from the blast. I yelled again and kicked him in the head. "Get the fuck out of the truck and go check on the lieutenant!" He snapped back to reality, grabbed his gear, and bolted out of the truck. I popped back up out of the turret and observed Worley jogging back towards us and out of the dust. He was unscathed but holding his ears. When he got to the side of the truck, he looked up at me in the turret and with a broad grin screamed as loud as he could, "Looks like we're at war, boys!" He was bleeding from his ears.

We still have no idea how Worley had survived the blast. It was a goddamn miracle, given the size of the explosion. Worley had me inform battalion through Viper that we were fully immersed in battle and needed more combat power. The QRF was en route.

The fight had become a 360-degree battle. The IEDs had blocked our vehicular movement, so we needed to defend ourselves until the QRF arrived. Despite the patchy dead zone, as the RTO, I knew I had to dismount and construct a field expedient directional antenna to force radio waves directly towards battalion HQ and hope they'd get our full transmissions. It was only a matter of time until Viper had to leave again and we needed a secure, guaranteed line of communications with HQ. Our ability to transmit and receive was still poor. I observed an old bombed-out Iraqi communications tower in the middle of a farm field about 150 yards to the west of our trucks. The tower was almost directly between the enemy fighters and us. It was the highest location in the area by far and really our only option to get the signal out. I saw an old, abandoned truck near the tower and some vegetation under it that could provide cover. Just get there, I said to myself. I pointed to the tower; Worley nodded, so I grabbed the radio and my weapon, and we ran fast and hard.

About halfway across the field, bullets began whizzing over us and kicking gravel and dirt up in our path. I was used to enemy fire hitting our trucks, but bullets tracking me on foot was new to me. Adrenaline immediately surged through our veins as we ran faster and harder than ever before. We breathlessly made it to the tower and Worley scanned the area for enemy fighters, while I assembled the antenna, grabbed a nearby rock, tied it to 550 cord and began trying to throw it up and over the highest portion of the tower. No luck. Suddenly, an AQI element unleashed a heavy volume of fire in our direction. I dropped to the ground and crawled back into some cover. I was pissed that I hadn't accomplished the task and felt I was letting everyone down. At that moment I felt more pressure than I ever had in my life.

Fortunately, the team on the ground to the south of us was watching over us and began suppressing the enemy firing at us. I got on my knees and threw a perfect hook shot over the beam. I quickly got the radio up and running and began speaking clearly with Major Morgan. Between transmissions, Worley and I engaged the enemy fighters who were now in an interlocking sector of fire between Crispen's team and us. The two

Apaches that were still on station were hammering the enemy in multiple locations. We were flipping the script and turning the tide.

Morgan informed us the QRF was a few minutes out and consisted of a platoon-size element, which included the battalion commander, four gun trucks, and two more Apaches. Haycock had made good time by not stopping to clear the road. He was being guided by one of the Apaches to search for IEDs using their technology and hoping most of the triggermen were now behind a gun fighting us and not waiting to detonate bombs. Morgan, meanwhile, was developing a picture in the assault command post, trying to determine what was unfolding outside of the combat zone. What we did not know was that Morgan and Haycock were using our new initiative as a means to exploit killing more of the enemy.

Once the QRF was within radio range, Major Morgan used ISR to coordinate a linkup so the battalion commander would be in direct contact with him to free up Worley to command his men in the fight. Worley maneuvered us south to meet up with the team who had now bandaged up the wounded soldiers from the HBIED and were reorganizing for an offensive maneuver west. Haycock directed the Viper element to provide route reconnaissance and close combat aviation support for us. The AH-64s immediately began picking up targets and engaging enemy fighters west and south of our location.

Suddenly, we heard another huge explosion to the north, followed up with a high volume of machine-gun fire. The QRF had been hit by an IED and were in an ambush. Haycock came up on the radio and informed us they had sustained no injuries or damage to the vehicles and were simply driving on through. They observed the triggermen running from the strike and knocked them down with machine-gun fire. AQI was now getting hit from multiple angles and only had one escape route—to the west. We were beating the hell out of them now.

The commander and operations officer saw our momentum. Haycock established communication with both Worley and Morgan. Worley had the close fight; Morgan had the deep, rear fight. We would move forward, engage targets, and maneuver farther west, while Haycock's QRF remained far enough back to not get decisively engaged with the enemy. Haycock wanted to keep the QRF reactionary to offer support at the right moment. The Apaches conducted gun runs to the north and south, ripping into the reed lines and palm groves, destroying anything protecting any enemy fighters hiding there.

We continued our push west along Fatboy until SPC Hursey climbed across a small canal on the north side of the road and yelled, "Stop movement!" He had discovered a daisy-chained IED on the road, consisting of four artillery shells stretched down the road for approximately 40–50 meters and spaced perfectly to hit our gun trucks or a dismounted platoon-sized patrol.

Corporal Zamora, the assistant team leader, pulled us off the road, forcing us to skirt between the road and some houses. As we re-gathered our momentum, the AQI fighters detonated the IED, probably as a diversion so they could escape. No causalities on our side. We were closing in on the enemy, engaging fighters who were running westward only a couple hundred yards in front of us. We were caught up in the chase and did not realize just how far we had extended ourselves from the trucks and communication.

Major Morgan overheard our chatter about the explosion and our plan to keep pushing west with our limited resources to kill or capture more fighters. He immediately ordered our patrol to stop all forward movement and told us to set up a perimeter. Our blood boiled! We had them on the run and were taking their terrain. The order didn't make sense.

Morgan, in coordination with the battalion commander, maneuvered a Viper element to track multiple enemy fighters. The Shadow UAV had found an enemy linkup point in a cemetery about five kilometers from our position. Morgan informed the battalion commander that Worley would hold his position so they could figure out a plan of attack. Whether the enemy was mounted up in a couple trucks to give the impression they were fleeing or whether they were simply baiting us into an ambush, we had no idea.

Morgan used the drone to guide the battalion commander's QRF south, directly towards the enemy position. We heard massive gunfire from gun trucks following the loud thumping of Apache helicopters. Haycock and Morgan had actually baited the enemy into their own ambush site. Our QRF had intercepted the AQI element preparing to ambush us. The QRF ended up killing the bulk of the AQI fighters, recovered enemy weapons and materiel, and Garmin global positioning devices, which exposed other enemy positions. The fighting had ended for the day, but the operation was just beginning.

Unlike most firefights, the battle had lasted approximately an hour. An AAR estimated that there were approximately 30–35 fighters attacking us from all directions. Approximately, a dozen enemy had been killed, more than a dozen wounded, and a half-dozen captured. We had only sustained minor injuries attributed to concussions from IED blasts or abrasions from debris.

The next day, we started clearing houses and found numerous HBIEDs. The region was littered with layer upon layer of IEDs implanted in the roads. We also found a major munitions arsenal near the radio tower where we had set up our radio during the fight. The truck we had used for cover was next to a firetruck inside an old chicken coop. Next to the firetruck was a car that was loaded down with explosives being prepared as a VBIED. We found dozens of artillery shells, mortars, rifles, machine guns, and IED-making materials buried in caches around the tower. The firetruck was also being wired up as a VBIED. We even found a few 500-pound aviation bombs. We had undoubtedly located the largest cache in the region at the time. It was a huge blow to AQI and Zarqawi.

This success focused Haycock to direct the battalion to execute ongoing missions to locate caches of bombmaking material. Morgan recalled, "We wanted the enemy to bleed from the heart and their bank account." The more we took from the enemy in materials, the more they had to expend resources to replace their losses. We also learned from tactical questioning of captured fighters that Zarqawi was paying locals to detonate IEDs. He even got them to film the blasts so he could post the kills on social media. That's when we learned that the enemy referred to us "Black Hearts"—and that we were relentless.

Although killing the enemy brings a sense of victory or payback, many times the best success is the capture of enemy fighters to gain crucial intelligence. Zarqawi had now gotten himself labeled as the most wanted man in the world and a ton of American assets were now hunting him.

Strike Force was in his backyard now. We thought we had gained the upper hand, but soon realized Zarqawi had a seemingly endless supply of money and motivated foreign fighters stretching from the Middle East through Europe and into North Africa to keep up his campaign against us.

Zarqawi rushed fighters from Fallujah and Ramadi into the region to stop our advance and maintain his freedom of movement into Baghdad. He desperately needed the southern access corridor, now obstructed by the Strike Brigade. Ambushes were getting more violent and complex with AQI hoping they could get us to break contact and go back to BIAP like the previous unit had done. Car bombs were detonating in Baghdad at a staggering rate. AQI was being more brazen in open confrontation versus the usual hit-and-run tactics. We were clearly disrupting their operations and Zarqawi was escalating the fight. We were in the right place and kicking the shit out of the hornets' nest.

CHAPTER 7

"Blue on Blue:" The Chaos and Confusion of War

On November 23, 2nd Platoon conducted a reconnaissance mission to locate another large cache of weapons and explosive material. This patrol was going further west of the cemetery where the insurgents used to meet, which we had discovered earlier that month during the second attack on Route Motorhead. Alpha Company had gained a foothold in the enemy's safe haven and the battalion was maintaining the offensive momentum. Our company had been conducting nonstop operations with four soldiers killed and over a dozen seriously wounded within three weeks of assuming control of the area. This casualty count was just our company. Every single patrol that left the base knew that it was guaranteed they would either find an IED, be hit by an IED, or find themselves in a gunfight. The operational tempo and combat stress was mounting.

The platoon loaded up in the dark and conducted pre-combat checks and inspections (PCCs/PCIs). Our sergeants were ruthless in this task. PCC/PCIs were vital to success in combat. Staff Sergeant Bass and Sergeant Meeuwsen of 2nd Platoon enforced exceptional standards and discipline among their soldiers and were highly regarded as leaders.

Bass had left the Marine Corps to join the Army. Meeuwsen had grown up in a military family. They were prime examples of highly disciplined soldiers who performed at the highest level. Their platoon leader, Lieutenant "Hank" was also considered one of the best platoon leaders in the battalion. This platoon was tough, gritty, and cohesive just like their platoon sergeant, SFC Geleney.

They deployed before dawn under blackout orders, reaching the southern portion of our AO as the sun rose. At the release point, teams dismounted from their gun trucks to patrol the area on foot to avoid IED attacks and better infiltrate the area towards the objective. Bass and Meeuwsen's patrol consisted of a 12-man-sized element that included an interpreter and Doc Ray, our combat medic. The patrol dismounted in the general area where our patrol had come under heavy fire on November 13. Lieutenant Hank led the patrol west down Route Fatboy and directly passed the location where AQI had tried to hit us with the daisy-chained IEDs.

The sun began peeking through the clouds, creating rays of light shining across the crops in the fields. The scene was one of subsistence living in what could be a place of friendliness and serenity, something straight out of the Bible, like the Garden of Eden, which, oddly enough, is where we were. It was a very quiet morning. Birds could be heard waking up, dogs were barking in the distance, mist was rising off the canal, but no signs of human life. Lieutenant Hank recognized that no one was working in the fields. The hair on everyone's neck rose. As always, this was never a good sign. Something was wrong.

Suddenly heavy machine-gun and small-arms fire shattered the early morning silence, ripping through the patrol. Lieutenant Hank ordered the patrol to immediately return fire and assault toward the enemy. They were being fired on from a house within yards of their position. In seconds, Bass and Meeuwsen began maneuvering their formations against the enemy, toward the house. Hank was struck in the left shoulder. The force of the round knocked him off his feet, tossing him backwards to the ground. Reacting to an ambush demands that you fight through until you get out of the kill zone, then consolidate and reorganize. You cannot stop and take care of casualties in a kill zone. Bass and Meeuwsen led the assault into the building, forcing the enemy to flee out of the back door. Once inside the structure, they quickly moved to the roof and started firing at the retreating enemy fighters.

Bass took the RTO to the roof while Doc Ray attended to Hank. Bass needed to push out a situation report (SITREP) to the company and battalion HQ. Unfortunately, as soon as they reached the roof, the antenna on the radio was shot in two and disabled. The squad found themselves in a serious firefight, greatly outnumbered, and without communication. They contacted their gun trucks via squad radios for support, but due to the canals, the trucks could not maneuver into supporting positions. All the soldiers back at the trucks could do was relay back to HQ and inform them that troops were in contact, then sit and hope their men returned while listening to the intense gunfight. Some of the soldiers in the trucks started planning a rescue mission that would have consisted of four of them teaming up. But Bass and Meeuwsen, although outnumbered, were calm and controlling the fight. They were confident attack aviation wasn't far off and did not think a last-resort effort of a rescue from their mounted unit was as yet needed. Such a rescue would mean that that only four guys would be left to defend the four trucks.

Bass realized they needed to gain fire superiority. The goal was to inflict a few casualties, forcing AQI to flee or bound backwards to care for their casualties. SPC Abels, a rifleman in the squad, and Bass, slowed down their rate of fire and began to knock down numerous enemy fighters by systematically targeting and eliminating the most serious threats. Hank was in bad shape and needed to be evacuated. Abels noticed a blue pickup truck outside the building.

"Let's take that truck."

"Negative," Bass said. "We don't have the keys."

"I'll check it out." Abels climbed down from the roof and ran out of the building, exposing himself to enemy fire. He busted the driver-side window open with his M4 and under fire, he hotwired the truck and yelled for the rest of the patrol, who placed Hank in the back of the truck, along with Abels, Doc Ray, and the Iraqi interpreter. Doc Ray and the interpreter took turns maintaining pressure on Hank's gunshot wound. Meeuwsen took the wheel while Bass returned fire from the passenger window. Meeuwsen floored the gas pedal as the patrol returned fire from all directions. They then headed east to a road intersection, back towards the gun trucks.

Just east of the ambush, 3rd Platoon was conducting a reconnaissance patrol to identify potential locations for a patrol base; the platoon could hear gunfire, but they did not know what was unfolding to their west. Due to the lost communications in 2nd Platoon, 3rd Platoon had no idea that 2nd Platoon was out in the AO and under attack. They started slowly rolling west towards the gunfight, trying to identify who was firing on whom.

Suddenly, one of the platoon gunners from the 3rd Platoon yelled, "Blue Bongo truck coming at us fast! About 1,000 meters. Weapons!" They had no idea that the blue Bongo truck contained men from the 2nd Platoon patrol. All 3rd Platoon knew was they were in enemy territory, a firefight had just occurred, and a blue Bongo pickup truck, known for being VBIEDs, was racing towards them with silhouetted people who appeared to have rifles. The order was given to engage the truck.

One gunner, using a .50-caliber machine gun, and the other, using a .240-caliber machine gun, released several bursts of gunfire on the advancing truck. The rounds sliced through the glass and metal with ease, striking Bass and Meeuwsen inside the cab. They were killed instantly. Hank was hit six more times. Abels was struck nine times, which almost completely severed his right arm. Doc Ray was hit once in the leg.

The truck veered off the road and crashed into the canal. As Hank explained later, he was unable to see anything. Believing they had been ambushed again by AQI fighters, and knowing other men were down, he rolled out of bed of the truck and over the side into the canal. As he laid there alone and bleeding out, he prepped a grenade and held it closely to his body. He was mentally prepared to use it on himself while killing enemy combatants.

When 3rd Platoon maneuvered towards the truck, they saw American military uniforms. They were devastated. U. S. soldiers had engaged their brothers in what we call "blue-on-blue," aka friendly fire. It's horrible when something like this happens, but it's even worse when they're the men you have lived with, trained with, and spent time with back home. We conducted a medical evacuation of our wounded and fallen heroes. After we had consolidated all our equipment and accounted for each other, we returned to FOB Striker. It was a crushing defeat. Being killed by the enemy is bad enough but being killed by your own is unimaginably painful.

Due to the complexity of the operations and terrain, platoon missions had to check in and submit a patrol "ticket," so the battalion could confirm fire control measures and allocate ISR resources and priority commitment for the QRF if needed. The operations center had been tracking the reconnaissance mission for the cache site near the AQI cemetery, but not the reconnaissance mission for the future patrol base. It was later determined that the company command post had postponed one of the missions and had not informed battalion. As a result, both missions went out on November 23 in close proximity to each other. When communications went down, there was no way to alert HQ that there was a serious ambush in progress.

Later that evening, Lieutenant Colonel Haycock and Major Morgan came by the company CP. Haycock met with Captain Donaldson one-on-one. While the battalion and company commander spoke privately, Major Morgan spent time with the company radio operators. He sat down and asked questions about what was going on in their minds. He commiserated with the loss we all felt. Morgan shared some of his experiences in firefights to help us understand the realities of combat.

For Haycock and Morgan, they were trying to come to grips with balancing the mission with the loss of lives in the battalion. Haycock returned from his talk with the commander and shared his perspective of what goes on at higher HQs in times like these. Morgan said as he had listened closely to the radio transmissions between the company CP and 3rd Platoon and could tell that something was unfolding in a bad way. Something was not right. The reports were not clear and were missing information that normally would come over the radio during enemy contact. They were vague and indecisive, which was not normal. What was key was there was no mention of enemy activity or casualties. Morgan's instinct and experience had taken over and he had immediately cleared the operations center and called for the battalion commander. He privately told Haycock that he believed we had a fratricide incident. That evening we gained a better appreciation of our battalion leadership's responsibility, while they learned more about our company's complex situation on the battlefield.

Screaming Eagles waiting for their orders to assault Iraq in 2003. (Kelly Eads)

Strike Heart 2-502 badge (Battalion Facebook page, used with permission)

Alpha Co soldiers, Kholouris, Jackson, Leonard, Boyles and Geleney with 2-502 taking a minute for a photo op just prior to invading Iraq in 2003. (Kelly Eads)

CPT Morgan displaying his cool new tool for war during the 2003 invasion. (Dan Morgan)

2-502 before 2005 deployment. (Kelly Eads)

Alpha Co, 2-502, prior to deployment in 2005. (Kelly Eads)

Alpha Co at Camp Stryker, Iraq, prior to full control in fall 2005. (Kelly Eads)

CPT Donaldson and 1SG Tessar meeting prior to an air assault training exercise at Fort Polk in 2005. (Kelly Eads)

PFC Byler showing off the "Old Abe" patch. (Kelly Eads)

PFC Byler getting promoted to Specialist and earning his "Blood Pins." (Kelly Eads)

1SG Tessar giving some final words of encouragement and advice prior to kicking off full combat operations. (Kelly Eads)

Strike Soldiers, Alpha Co, 2-502, headed south down Route Motorhead before a complex ambush attack only moments later where they survived 14 IED strikes in 45 minutes. (Kelly Eads)

PFC Gorton standing inside a "standard" IED crater left over after a strike on his patrol. (Kelly Eads)

Scouts 2-502 take a moment to get a photo in while on some downtime in 2006. (Kelly Eads)

SSG Bievre, KIA in early 2006. (Kelly Eads)

Aviation bomb located in a cache. (Kelly Eads)

A moment of peace and beauty as the sun set on a late evening while manning "the gun." (Kelly Eads)

Mortar section returning fire on enemy locations. (Kelly Eads)

HHC Mortar section, led by SSG Mora, maneuvers during Operation *Glory Light.* (Kelly Eads)

Gator Swamp's beginning stages and construction, already being riddled with bullet holes. (Kelly Eads)

SGT Sullivan and PFC Gorton working on improving defensive positions on top of Gator Swamp. (Kelly Eads)

Eagle Dustoff rescue medical aircraft picking up wounded Iraqi and American soldiers after an IED strike on Alpha Co patrol. (Kelly Eads)

"The Pain Gang," from left to right, SFC Walker and LT Worely from 3rd Platoon, SFC Geleney and LT "Hank" from 2nd Platoon. (Kelly Eads)

CPT George Morris directs troops in contact during an air assault operation to target Al Qaeda leadership, 2007. (Battalion Facebook page)

101st Airborne's aviation assets picking up soldiers. (Battalion Facebook page)

Soldiers conducting a low light operation to find, fix and target insurgents in Iraq. (Battalion Facebook page)

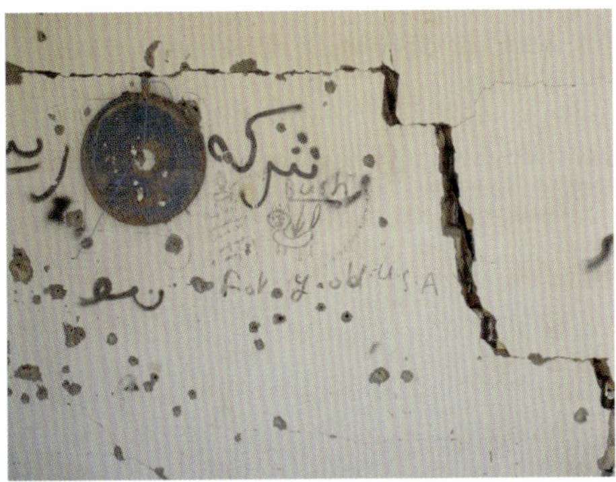

An Al Qaeda sniper training range in the Chakas with a message left for the Scouts in 2007. (Kelly Eads)

Al Qaeda weapons and equipment detailed after a Scout raid in 2007. (Kelly Eads)

Another type of pressure-button-activated IED located on foot patrol placed to target Scouts while on recon patrol in Chakas. (Kelly Eads)

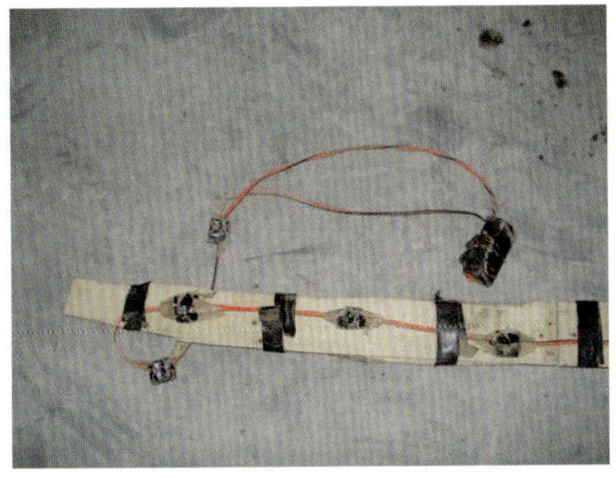

One of many pressure plate initiators for an IED found by Scouts in 2007. (Kelly Eads)

Scouts SSG Eads and PFC Engel at a school near the Tigris River (2008). (Kelly Eads)

Recovered Al Qaeda in Iraq and Syria flag belonging to some of the first organized ISIS fighters in 2008 (Chaka operation). (Kelly Eads)

Items located in a cache that was used to attack soldiers and Iraqi police near Fob Kalsu in 2007–08. (Kelly Eads)

SFC Overway with C Co, 2-502, and later Scouts, directing his platoon during the Chaka clearance. (Kelly Eads)

SFC Whitted, later the CSM for 2-502, taking some time out of his patrol to connect with a local child and share a little American love and candy. Encounters like these took operations to the next level. (Battalion Facebook page)

Markets in Mahawil open for the day, 2008. (Kelly Eads)

SGT Spear with the Scouts, taking some time with children of a family who had just been attacked by an Al Qaeda suicide bomber—the aftermath of that attack can be seen in the background (2007). This photo speaks a thousand words. (Kelly Eads)

SPC Betts with Scouts setting up his overwatch position. (Kelly Eads)

Elements of Recon Team 2 and the sniper team taking a breather. (Kelly Eads)

SSG Eads, CPL Ammerman, and CPL Spear. (Kelly Eads)

Scouts, from left to right, SSG Arnold, SPC Rahn, Interpreter Ox and LT Stephens, relaxing during some downtime during an operation to target an extreme Shia Special Group/Hit Squad (2007–08). The scouts killed the leader of the squad while en route to their overwatch positions—sort of carrying out the operation backwards. (Kelly Eads)

Specialist Rowlands pulling security during the Chaka clearance. (Kelly Eads)

Members of the Mahawil Emergency Response Team 2007, their version of an American SWAT Team. (Kelly Eads)

Scouts from Recon Team One from left to right PFC Engel, SSG Eads, and SPC Stauch (2007–08). (Kelly Eads)

Scout snipers from left to right, PFC Coey, SGT Alexanders, and SPC Martinez (2007–08). (Kelly Eads)

Scouts Recon Team 3, left to right, PVT Ohman, SPC Tate, SSG Sullivan, PVT Rowlands, SGT Spear, and PVT Brewster (2007–08). (Kelly Eads)

LT Stephens looking at an IED that targeted him but missed by just feet as he crossed the bridge towards the IED behind him. There is visible damage to the barriers beside him—it was a very close call. (Kelly Eads)

An IED that struck the Scouts on Christmas Day 2007. Luckily there were no injuries, meaning it was a very Merry Christmas! (Kelly Eads)

SPC Rowlands and SPC Rhan setting in a defensive posture during clearance of the Chakas. (Kelly Eads)

Scouts taking hold of an extreme outpost that was attacked and nearly overrun (2010–11). (Battalion Facebook page)

Strike and 101st soldiers conducting insert and exfil training. (Battalion Facebook page)

Strike soldiers conducting low-light operations in an open field. (Battalion Facebook page)

Scouts training with United States Marine aviation assets. (Battalion Facebook page)

2-502 Scouts posing in front of a 160th SOAR MH-47 after a joint training operation. (Battalion Facebook page)

Memorial for Operation *Iraqi Freedom* 2005–07. (Facebook Webpage)

Memorial for Operation *Iraqi Freedom* 2007–2009. (Facebook Webpage)

Memorial for Operation *Enduring Freedom* 2010–2011. (Facebook Webpage)

Annual Veterans Day memorial, 101st Airborne Division Headquarters (Facebook Webpage)

CHAPTER 8

Patrol Base Gator Swamp

After the fratricide of November 23, the battalion directed a safety stand-down for the company to refit and manage battle fatigue and stress. We had only been responsible for our area for just under two months and had had six soldiers killed and more than two dozen wounded. We spent time sleeping, playing cards, working out, and meeting with counselors. We were shellshocked, but we were still motivated and cohesive as a unit. The days started to drag and, although we appreciated the reprieve, we wanted to get back into the fight.

We were back in action in early December 2005. The company mounted up and commenced operations back down Motorhead. We needed to find a patrol base to have a 24/7 presence and manage our operational tempo better. The patrol leaders received specific requirements. The patrol base needed 1) observation positions for early warning, 2) clear fields of fire, 3) ingress and egress routes, 4) a hardened structure with elevated positions, and 5) to be large enough for six to eight UAHs and up to 50 warriors. During our two weeks' stand-down, the company and battalion leadership analyzed all the intelligence from past operations and incoming intelligence from local and national reconnaissance assets over our area. The intelligence officer determined that we needed to do a specific bridge reconnaissance while looking for a patrol base because it was the only crossing point that would allow us to get after the enemy farther south. Due to thick vegetation cover, ISR aircraft and other air support could not find it.

The bridge was a key terrain feature being used by AQI to cross the canal network to infiltrate north to Baghdad and attack us. The enemy needed this bridge to transport IEDs, fighters and supplies, and VBIEDs into Baghdad. Captain Donaldson tasked Staff Sergeant Skurzewski from 3rd Platoon to locate and assess the bridge.

For the first couple weeks of December, the entire company had been rotating through the area while trying to find this critical bridge. Sergeant Skurzewski's team consisted of half of 3rd Platoon and was labeled Crew 1. They were mainly checking out the far end of Route Motorhead as a location for a patrol base and determined that no IED explosions or other enemy activity had taken place there since the November 13 attack.

Staff Sergeant Crispen's team, the other half of 3rd Platoon, Crew 2, returned to the area and checked out the surrounding houses because they were strangely abandoned, despite being well maintained. They discovered IED-making materials in a few houses, which led to the conclusion that the structures were being prepped as HBIEDs. The patrol confirmed this assumption after they detained three AQI suspects while on a foot patrol, both of whom tested positive for explosive residue on their hands. It was very clear that AQI had not given up on the location.

Days later, Crew 1 went to the cemetery and were investigating the area for potential IED and weapon caches when suddenly the battalion HQ tasked them with assisting an Apache element in containing and detaining two Bongo trucks with suspected AQI fighters. Initial reports from the Apache element were that these personnel seemed to have AK-47s and RPGs in the vicinity of a school south of 3rd Platoon's location.

The battalion wanted the patrol to rapidly move five to seven kilometers back southeast to the suspected terrorists' location without clearing the road first. Skurzewski calmly responded, "Negative" and requested the Apache gunships engage the enemy while his patrol move safely southward. Upon arrival at the engagement site, the patrol would conduct site exploitation and battlefield damage assessment.

The battalion operations center came back on the radio and stated the Apache element was not comfortable with engaging the armed personnel because they had not been shot at themselves. That was one of the ROE for the aviation units. This refusal foreshadowed the future challenges we would have with this specific aviation unit to support us during troops-in-contact missions. The Apaches would not engage clearly armed terrorists in a terrorist hotbed unless they were fired on or were requested to fire on enemy forces by a ground force who'd make the call for the attack.

Skurzewski directed the Apache element to provide route reconnaissance ahead of his patrol, along with ISR technology from the battalion, so they could move quicker to the terrorists' location and intercept them. The Apaches' technology was so advanced that one helicopter could maintain a high-enough position from miles away to keep an eye on enemy fighters without them knowing, while the other aircraft provided low route clearance. It remained high risk, regardless of the Apache presence, because this was Route Fatboy, a known hot spot littered with IEDs and enemy fighters. As the patrol approached a turn near a school, an IED detonated in front of the trail vehicle. As the dust settled and amidst the radio chatter to determine casualties, the gunner of the lead vehicle yelled, "Found the bridge." Strange things happen in combat. No one was wounded and they had found the critical bridge.

Soldiers bailed out of the trail vehicle and did a quick individual recon of potential secondary IEDs, which we called "5 and 25s." This technique required a soldier to scan five to 25 meters around him as opposed to reacting too quickly and blindly running into a secondary IED. The dismounted squad found copper wire and traced it back to the triggerman's position. He had been hiding in a two-house complex north of the bridge. The other two vehicles were already in a herringbone formation at the bridge, effectively blocking any enemy vehicle from maneuvering across the bridge. The rest of the patrol, minus the gunners and drivers, dismounted and converged on the house complex. As they searched the complex, they determined from the tire tracks that the triggerman had jumped in a vehicle and fled the scene south across the bridge, likely towards the school as based on the information from the Apache element.

The Apaches had guided the patrol into a coordinated attack but refused to engage the enemy despite positive identification of their activity and weapons, and an IED attack. It was clearly a hostile situation that met the engagement criteria. They also informed the patrol that they had to break station just after the IED explosion because they were low on fuel. As they departed, they confirmed that the enemy had consolidated south of the school about 200 meters away.

As the patrol prepared to cross the bridge, the school let the children out for the day. The enemy were using the school as a safe haven and yet had still attacked the patrol within a few hundred meters of these kids. The patrol needed to cross the bridge and turn left past the school and stop at the next intersection, where they would be able to cut off the enemy on a dead-end road. As they passed the school, Sergeant Martin, one of the team leaders, spotted shiny copper wire in the sunlight about 50 meters in front. The wire led to the back of the school and to an oddly located cemetery mausoleum. Skurzewski yelled, "IED!" and ordered the patrol to stop. Sergeant First Class Walker, the patrol leader, directed the platoon to cordon the area and directed Sergeant Skurzewski to clear the school for enemy personnel before moving forward.

The rest of the patrol dismounted from the vehicles, minus a couple gunners, and approached the double door of the school courtyard. It was locked, which was not unexpected since a fucking bomb had just gone off. SFC Walker floored the gas pedal of the gun truck and rammed the flimsy wooden door. The patrol cleared the school and apparently found no indications of AQI inside. As they exited the one school building and moved along the exterior school wall towards the mausoleum out back, they found additional wires coming from a window inside another building in the school courtyard. There they could see two AQI fighters huddled together inside.

Sergeant Martin had the interpreter inform the two fighters that they had nowhere to go and needed to surrender or they would start throwing grenades into the room. The two enemy personnel surrendered and slowly came out of the structure, dropped their AK-47s, ammo bandoliers, and the detonator to the IED. The interpreter pointed out that one of the guys was not Iraqi, but a foreign fighter from Saudi Arabia.

After taking the pair into custody, the patrol consolidated and moved back to the house complex on the northern side of the bridge and set up a defense perimeter. SFC Walker wanted further guidance from the battalion command. The battalion directed them to defend in place while the battalion brought down a route-clearance platoon to clear the roads in the area. Our 2nd Platoon would accompany the route-clearance team and EOD personnel. Then, both platoons would return to base with the route-clearance team upon completion, along with the two captured fighters.

As the hours passed, SFC Walker analyzed the area and realized that they had discovered a solid location for a patrol base. The complex was two stories high with a walled compound. The rooftop gave 360-degree observation with expansive, clear fields of fire, that controlled the bridge only 20 meters to the front and which was near the school. There's no better way to win over the local population than through the children.

★

After returning to base, Walker got approval from HQ to establish the patrol base on Route Fatboy about a mile west from Route Motorhead. We named it "Gator Swamp" after our Alpha Company's radio call sign, Gator.

We had been fighting in the area for weeks. Control of the bridge and the school gave us added protection and increased our freedom of movement. But we had miscalculated the enemy's need to take back this strategic bridge location. With no concern for civilians, the enemy began targeting us with every weapon they had—mortars, sniper fire, and IEDs.

Gator Swamp was enclosed by a thick six-foot-tall brick wall. The front gate faced south towards the bridge and the school across the canal. The base required large convoys of materials, ammunition, and equipment to fortify the location. We needed to defend ourselves 24/7, while conducting frequent offensive operations. This place would be perfect.

We immediately set up fighting positions with heavy machine guns on every corner of the rooftop. The battalion required us to carry sandbags and a couple sheets of plywood in the trucks just in case we needed to remain forward and conduct hasty defensive positions in a building. We put that plywood and hundreds of sandbags in position to protect the gunners. For now, the sandbags would help stop incoming rounds and shrapnel from rockets and mortars.

Since we were now in enemy territory and among the local populace, the enemy's early warning network was at a disadvantage. We could now exit the patrol base silently on foot at night and maneuver into position for whatever the mission required at the time—ambushes, blocking positions, reconnaissance, and kill or capture missions. We owned the night. Gator Swamp gave us flexibility which in turn put AQI on their heels. The enemy now had to operate round the clock and their positional advantage was deteriorating.

Almost from the beginning, AQI leadership targeted Gator Swamp. They began by studying us as we improved our defenses, rotated our platoons in and out of the base, and conducted offensive operations. The base defense was tested on a daily basis by mortar and sniper fire.

We kept improving the defensive perimeter, by burning the reed line to the north of the base and to the south near the bridge in order to open up fields of fire and destroy AQI cover along the canals. Each time our men attempted to improve outside defenses they would come under heavy harassing fire.

In late December, 3rd Platoon deployed from Gator Swamp to install Jersey barriers along the southern end of Route Mortorhead and along Route Fatboy, the road that led directly to Gator Swamp. Jersey barriers are concrete stands about three feet high and eight feet long. We'd place them in a serpentine formation to force vehicles to slow down. The effort was a multi-day, 24/7 effort—slow, cumbersome, and risky. The platoon integrated razor-sharp concertina wire throughout the serpentine to ensure no high-speed VBIED could get close the patrol base. These barriers extended south down Motorhead and then east along Fatboy for hundreds of yards. We took every precaution and utilized every resource in Class IV materials supplied by Army logistics.

We left the patrol base to link up with the large Army trucks transporting the Jersey barriers. This mission, to emplace the barriers, required two platoons, which left behind approximately a dozen soldiers to defend Gator Swamp. Within minutes of our departure, all hell broke loose. AQI fighters attacked the base with RPGs, resulting in serious structural damage, chaos, and a half-dozen friendly WIAs. SFC Walker informed the battalion that the patrol base was under attack while team leaders were roused from sleep and other duties to man all fighting positions. Normally, in a firefight you do not want to give up your heavy machine-guns' position, but at this point, the RPGs kept coming and shrapnel, bits of rock and metal, were zinging everywhere.

We needed to regain fire superiority. The machine-gunners engaged immediately but quickly started taking the heavier fire. Calls for ammo rang out in between heavy volumes of fire from our machine guns. Dust and dirt saturated the inside of the base structure. Machine gunner PFC Applewhite came stumbling down the steps yelling for a medic due to shrapnel wounds all over his body. Private Packer and Private Heatherly immediately dashed past him, knowing he had left his position on the roof and took positions on the southern side of the wall where they started suppressing enemy fire. Sergeant Skurzewski reached the roof a short time later as dozens of red tracer rounds slammed into the side of the building, spitting concrete fragments all over the place.

Skurzewski suddenly noticed a pair of feet frantically kicking near the southern end of the roof. He ran through the door, managing to avoid a barrage of enemy gunfire, and found Private Packer hunched down over PFC Heatherly, shielding him from incoming bullets that were slamming inches above them.

Packer yelled to Skurzewski, "Heatherly's been shot in the head, goddamnit!"

Heatherly was screaming, "My head, my head!"

Skurzewski, fearing the worst and seeing a large amount of blood coming from under the helmet, unsnapped the helmet chinstrap thinking it was the only thing holding Heatherly's head together. He carefully took the helmet off and began searching his head for a wound. He found that the round had pierced Heatherly's helmet, followed the inside rim, scoring his scalp, and exited out the back, but had never actually penetrated the skull. Skurzewski informed Heatherly that he was okay and Heatherly responded with a thumbs-up. Once the medic showed up and bandaged his wound, Heatherly grabbed a rifle and kept on fighting.

The sounds of the heavy thumping of Apache gunships cut through the dense, humid air. As soon the Viper element arrived on scene the enemy shifted their fire from the patrol base to the Apaches. The lead Apache took dozens of hits, forcing the gunships to immediately break contact before they had even had a chance of firing a single round, rocket, or missile. With the enemy focused on the Apaches, our soldiers seized the opportunity and began raining bullets and mortars on target locations.

A second Apache team came on station in direct support of us. As they were inbound, we radioed the grid location of the enemy and marked our frontline trace and patrol base with smoke in order for the Apaches to quickly identify us. The new set of pilots wasted no time and came in hot, lighting up the enemy with 30mm machine-gun fire and Hellfire missiles. They unleashed everything they had and came up on the radio to say they were "black" on ammo, meaning they had expended all their ammunition. So, the Apache loitered in the area providing surveillance until a third Apache team arrived on station. For the next 15 to 20 minutes, the Apache pilots reconnoitered the area and identified enemy movement so we could target them with mortars from the base. The enemy eventually broke contact. We had won another tough battle but, again, we were surprised with their tenacity to fight it out as opposed to their usual hit-and-run tactics.

A couple hours later our battlefield damage assessment (BDA) revealed numerous AQI fighters had been wounded or killed, but no bodies had been left behind. We found what appeared to be several enemy casualty collection points, but they cared for each other like we did for our own: they had triaged the wounded, and quickly moved them out. We estimated 20–25 enemy fighters had attacked the base. It was an impressive attack, but our defensive preparations, close combat aviation integration, and leadership had saved the day.

Gator Swamp was now our home for months to come. We spent most of our time improving our defenses, ducking from incoming enemy fire and waiting for the next platoon to relieve us so we could go back to the main base.

On one patrol SPC Crider was able to trade some American goods for a goat. We stuffed the goat in the back of our truck and took him back to Gator Swamp. Upon arrival, the other guys asked where in the hell we got the goat and were laughing because they thought we had brought it back to the base as some kind of pet. Moments later there was a gunshot and the goat was dead. They didn't realize it had been brought back to be turned into fresh meat. A treat. We pooled together salt and pepper, Tabasco, and vegetables from our normal Meals, Ready-to-Eat (MREs) and cooked the meat on a homemade grill. It turned into one of the most memorable meals ever because it provided a brief respite from combat where we felt like we were home at a backyard BBQ.

It wasn't long until the next platoon was en route to relieve us. Every two to three weeks we rotated platoons so one platoon could go back to FOB Striker at BIAP to shower, work out, and call home. We always did relief in place and supply drops at night, but it was always risky because it required a lot of movement and, if not careful, predictability for the enemy. It was much easier at night to conceal our approach and decrease the possibility of a helicopter getting shot down, especially with troops on board.

As soon as we got word that relief was coming, we prepared our gear and readied to switch out platoons. We left a small group on the roof for security, while the rest of us moved to the LZ located in a large open field just outside the walls of base and laid in a ditch for our rides to show up.

We could hear two or three Black Hawks flying above the tree line headed our way. In front of them was one large CH-47 carrying personnel and sling-loading a large pallet of supplies on a heavy cable below it that would sustain the soldiers in the base for a couple of days. The CH-47 approached the LZ from the south. It was pitch dark. What the pilot must not have seen, or known, was that there were power lines that ran east–west right in front of the patrol base. As the pilot approached, he flew the sling load right though the powerlines. I was surprised that this had occurred because it was well known that these powerlines existed based on past flights and resupply missions.

The entire helicopter turned bright green through our night vision, and its blades glowed with electricity. We had all stepped up out of the ditch, preparing to load the Black Hawks once they landed; they were now on approach, but after seeing the CH-47 hit the lines, we dove back into the ditch, thinking the massive helicopter was about to explode or crash. Thankfully, the electrical charge disappeared just as quickly as it had appeared and the giant aircraft dropped off our supplies. The pilot controlled the aircraft like nothing had happened.

Shortly afterwards, we boarded the Black Hawks and were en route for a real shower, some better shitty food, and contact with families back home. As we approached the airfield we noticed a slight glow through our night vision, and, as we got closer, saw that the chow hall was on fire. Then we noticed our tents, which were only a couple hundred feet away from the chow hall, had burned to the ground as well: hot ash had blown onto the tents. All of our sentimental items shipped to us from family and friends were gone. So much for resting and refitting. The fight continued.

★

In January 2006, we returned to Patrol Base Gator Swamp for the rest of the tour. We continued to defend against enemy fire. We went on night patrols to flush out and engage the enemy, and clear the roads. We were inspired that the Iraqi government had finally committed Iraqi Army forces to support us by manning security checkpoints along Motorhead.

During a brisk, sunny winter's day, a massive convoy departed FOB Striker to clear Route Motorhead and establish the permanent security checkpoints to keep it safe from enemy activity. It was a massive show of coalition combat power. The convoy was spearheaded by a Husky IED-seeking vehicle, which had a ground-penetrating radar to identify buried IEDs under asphalt or dirt. Captain Donaldson commanded the convoy from the second truck in the convoy, with me in the turret and Sergeant Vosbein driving.

We turned off Motorhead and were heading west on the asphalt road when trucks to the rear started taking sniper fire. We pulled over to allow the rest of the convoy to drive on by and went back to check on the soldiers being fired on. No one was hurt so we drove on to catch up with the convoy. While driving, we observed some freshly laid concrete in the middle of the road. The convoy, for some reason, had driven around it and had not reported anything suspicious. Captain Donaldson ordered us to halt and I got out on foot to search around the suspicious filled-in hole. Sergeant Vosbein jumped up into the gunner position to replace me as I grabbed my rifle and slowly walked up the side of the road towards the suspicious pad of concrete. The pad had no U.S. markings. I couldn't believe our EODs hadn't checked on it. I walked all the way up to it, and even stood on top of it. Nothing seemed out of place; if they had wanted to kill us, what a great opportunity for them with me literally standing on top of it. Suddenly, I was ordered to mount up. It had apparently been decided to clear the suspicious site on the way back with the radar on the engineer trucks.

A few hours later, on the way back to FOB Striker to drop off the other combat units and the Husky vehicle, I was now located near the front of the convoy, again behind my gun, scanning for any possible triggermen or other threats. We drove by the suspicious hole, which had now been passed twice by radar-searching trucks and EOD. As I scanned for possible enemy locations, a massive explosion went off behind me. I looked back to see a huge open-bed armored personnel carrier the size of a neighborhood garbage truck flipping effortlessly through the air then crashing down.

Iraqi soldiers being transported in the open bed were thrown through the air three or four stories high. If the explosion didn't kill them, the impact of hitting the ground did. We observed two figures running out of a house north towards a palm grove. We called for aviation support who tracked them until our soldiers could capture them.

All the American soldiers lunged out of the trucks and ran fearlessly towards the explosion to assist their fellow soldiers, Iraqi and American. The vehicle was being driven by a good friend of mine, Corporal Ketterling. I was torn inside and terrified to see what had happened to him. Fourteen Iraqi soldiers were dead or seriously maimed. Ketterling had been wearing his seatbelt and was alive, although he had some serious injuries to his back from the fall. The remaining Iraqi force of three or four trucks grabbed their dead and immediately left the area in fear, leaving just the American Strike Force battalion to protect the local citizens. We could not stop them from leaving the area or from fighting back. It was a setback because a primary objective was to get the Iraqi Army in control of the area to protect their fellow citizens. The attack left us alone again, protecting the Iraqis all by ourselves. We had sustained a massive IED attack right when we thought we had gained control over the roads and surrounding terrain. It reminded us that the enemy always had a vote.

CHAPTER 9

Operation Glory Light and its Aftermath

Alpha Company had penetrated due south into the heart of enemy territory. We had conducted dozens of air assaults over the past five months. We had made headway, taken terrain formerly held by AQI but the flow of weapons, IEDs, and enemy fighters continued to terrorize the region. It was time to marshal the full power of U.S. military assets in a major air and ground assault. The target was a large insurgent stronghold in Sadr Yusufiyah, located due west from Gator Swamp and north of the Russian power plant, along the Euphrates River. Its location provided a great waypoint for logistics and foreign fighters to refit and plan attacks against us and push into Baghdad. Sadr Yusufiyah was also a wealthy area, so we suspected it held significant financiers of the terrorist operations in and around Baghdad.

The Operation Glory Light objective was to pinch off the enemy by air assaulting due west, effectively surrounding AQI and cutting them off from Ramadi and Falluja. AQI fighters used both the roadways along the Euphrates River and the river itself to maneuver men, suicide bombers, money, and weapons. It gave them an option of avoiding roads and U.S. checkpoints. We aimed to take the area by surprise and to leave U.S. and Iraqi troops in place as we had done with Gator Swamp. This time, the main effort was spearheaded by our sister company, Charlie Company of 2-502nd, commanded by Captain Vigilante. We were about to commence one of the largest operations since the invasion of Iraq.

The plan was to conduct an air assault out of the Baghdad airport before dawn in total blackout mode, with hundreds of Black Hearts from both the 1st and 2nd Battalions of the 502nd, and our Iraqi counterparts from the 6th and 9th Iraqi Army Divisions aboard dozens of UH-60 Black Hawks and CH-47 Chinooks. Battalion ISR assets would have an eye on the target AO prior to our arrival, while Viper attack helicopters would guide and cover our movement on the way in. At the tail end was a simultaneous ground assault convoy consisting of IED-locating vehicles, M1 Abrams tanks, and BFVs, which would clear Route Caprice, the main avenue from BIAP into Sadr Yusufiyah, and which would provide a massive amount of firepower if needed, paving the way for all logistical equipment to follow.

It was awesome!

In the early morning hours of March 2, 2006, I was standing by on the tarmac of BIAP waiting for the order to load into a Black Hawk—the "birds." It was an awe-inspiring scene. There is something about helicopters and night operations that create a sense of anticipation and excitement. The smell of gas, hot humid air, the stench of Baghdad airport, and warriors kitted up for combat exemplified the image of belligerent men lined up waiting for their rides to go unleash violence.

The pilots throttled up the engines and the blades began churning in the humid pre-dawn air. Static electricity between the blades and the ground lit up the area like a flurry of sparklers on the 4th of July. Dozens of UH-60 Black Hawks in rows were growling with torque, loaded up with serials and chalks as far as the eye could see. Apache AH-64 Viper attack helicopters were circling overhead ready to lead the transports off. I could hear the crackling of hundreds of radios and commanders giving codewords to their men. NCOs were directing soldiers into posture to load.

One of the senior NCOs yelled out to Lieutenant Colonel Haycock and Major Morgan, "You're up! … The commander and the '3' are up! Time to go! Man up!"

It was our turn.

Even this early in the morning, and even while blacked out, the surface-to-air threat against the helicopters was real at BIAP, but this time, it went off without a hitch. Adrenaline was pumping as the battalion lifted off. I could only imagine how quickly the AQI information lines were blowing up, alerting each other of some kind of huge operation kicking off. Doors were open and we looked out over the horizon through our night vision optics illuminating the bright green landscape of the region below. The aircraft banked hard left and we headed southwest towards the enemy. Haycock and Morgan were hundreds of feet above us in a Black Hawk monitoring the operation's serials, chalks, multiple landing zones and the large ground assault convoy. They would stay airborne for hours, pissing in Gatorade bottles, directing the assault.

The Black Hawks screamed over at rooftop level in route to the LZ in order to reduce our signature and increase the element of surprise. We knew that as soon as we left BIAP, AQI would try to alert each other; this low-flying maneuver was a technique used to avoid or counter the threat of surface-to-air missiles (SAMs) or heavy machine guns. Lower-flying and fast-flying aircraft are harder to identify from the ground due to trees and buildings. Last, pilots could quickly drop troops at an LZ versus coming in from a higher altitude. The battalion usually conducted numerous false insertions in order to distract the enemy from our actual route and objective. This strategy was used to confuse AQI as to where troops were actually being dropped off. We were one minute away from our final approach to the LZ when the pilots began rapid chaffing countermeasures. Apparently, our aircraft had been "painted" with a laser-targeting system from an enemy SAM platform, kicking in the aircraft's warning systems and resulting in the pilots' countermeasure.

It was the first time most of us experienced this evasive technique used to draw enemy missile fire away from the chopper. Bright, loud, white flares exploded outwardly from the side of the aircraft, while the pilots banked hard right, catching everyone inside off guard. Many of us actually thought we had been hit by a missile or were experiencing some kind of engine failure. It was terrifying to say the least. The maneuver nearly resulted in a collision with another Black Hawk directly on our starboard. The blades of the other aircraft came within feet of our open door. Some of us could actually see our brothers' shocked expressions in the other aircraft. Even through night vision, I could clearly see the guys in the other aircraft grab on to parts of the helicopter and lean inside to brace for a collision. Fortunately, the pilots in the other Black

Hawk responded quickly and banked right as well. We landed seconds later without incident and continued with the mission.

Dozens of UH-60 Black Hawks were on the ground at this point, as hundreds of Strike Force Screaming Eagles jumped out. It was the pure controlled chaos of war. Within a few minutes, over 500 Screaming Eagles were advancing towards their objectives. The pilots lifted off and disappeared over the horizon into the night sky. In moments, it was silent. All you could hear were crackling radio conversations, soldiers whispering, and dogs barking in the distance.

Over the next few hours, all units came under sporadic mortar and small-arms fire. Fortunately, we had immediately established the battalion mortar firing points to support the operation. The mortar team, led by Staff Sergeant Mora, were some of the first men inserted into the battlespace and immediately began counterfire operations, destroying a few enemy mortar teams within a couple hours. One of the engagements was a mortar duel between the enemy and our mortar teams firing at each other. You could hear Staff Sergeant Mora for hundreds of yards as he screamed fire commands to motivate his mortarmen to win the fight. The mortar sections had been exchanging rounds back and forth for twenty minutes when suddenly Mora adjusted fire based on a crater analysis of an enemy round and launched a half a dozen mortar rounds. The enemy were killed in place and their tubes destroyed.

In the pre-dawn darkness, we had owned the battlefield thanks to our night vision technology. When the sun came up, the enemy came outside and found hundreds of Screaming Eagles and dozens of tanks and AFVs along the roads patrolling the area. After a brief attack, most enemy fighters realized what they were up against, so they dropped their weapons and ran back into the villages before we could capture them to blend in with the local populace. Most were eventually located and detained because they were foreigners and couldn't hide their accent. Those from the region were able to play it off as if they were from the community, but those unable to provide documentation that they lived in the area were detained and handed off to intelligence units.

The operation consisted of deliberate route clearances, house-to-house searches, and local leader meetings to explain the purpose of the operation.

Overall, the operation lasted for a week. There were, fortunately, only two IED attacks, and seven different sustained firefights. We detected and cleared 21 IEDs by EOD teams. We located two VBIEDs wired and prepared for movement to Baghdad and seized 15 weapon caches. We had 16 high-value targets in custody, dozens of lower-level fighters, and about a dozen enemy KIA. Zarqawi was reportedly to have had been there earlier but had made a quick escape upon our arrival. Even though we did not capture him, Operation Glory Light was deemed a success. Coalition forces now owned 90 percent of the enemy safe haven and had shut down many of their operations. Most of the terrain had never been occupied by U.S. forces.

A few days later, as we were settling back into more routine operations after Operation Glory Light, an AH-64 Apache from 4-4 Aviation Battalion, 4th Infantry Division was shot down not far from us, inside the Operation Glory Light AO. Elements from 1-502nd Infantry Battalion "First Strike," immediately launched quick-reaction forces to the area, but were held up by IEDs. Our battalion directed the battalion Scout Platoon to simultaneously ready themselves for an air assault to the crash site location as a contingency.

Within 30 minutes, our scouts reported they were wheels down at the crash site via UH-60 Black Hawks from BIAP. They secured the site and searched the nearby area for the pilots. Meanwhile, the QRF cleared through multiple IEDs and arrived on the scene. They eventually found the body of a pilot killed in the crash. The helicopter had been completely destroyed. Debris and weapons were strewn about all over the crash site. One of the scouts discovered a blood trail leading to a nearby road. The second pilot's body was found buried under debris from the crash.

Our standing orders were not to leave anything for the enemy. After the bodies of the two pilots were medevac'd back to the main base, we got to work. It took three days of multiple units using cranes, forklifts, wreckers, IED-clearance teams, security forces, and more to help with security and clean up the crash site.

The incident affected operations in our area. We had thought that after Glory Light, the region was secure. Everyone was concerned. Aircraft did not normally get shot down in Iraq. IEDs were a common threat, but SAM threats were to dramatically change the dynamics. The fight was not over.

Two weeks later the battalion conducted a combined operation with Special Operations Forces (SOF) that lasted three days. It was really the final roundup of an enemy stronghold containing the hardest enemy fighters left in our AO. Haycock and Morgan co-located to Gator Swamp to control the supporting operations, while providing additional combat power as a QRF unit. The SOF task force, who executed their operations independently of us, was rounding up dozens of enemy combatants and sympathizers. The area south of Gator Swamp, north of the Russian power plant, echoed with explosive breaches, rocket attacks, Minigun runs, and follow-on firefights. Attack helicopters made swooping turns and dives as they unleashed rockets and machine-gun fire into the enemy. It was amazing to see from the rooftop of Gator Swamp.

Lieutenant Colonel Haycock and Major Morgan stood on a bridge overlooking the battlefield directing attack aviation and ISR to support the Strike Force battalion assisting in the fight. Our mission was to provide an outer layer of security to prevent enemy reinforcements from entering the battlespace and attacking the SOF task force, as well as killing or capturing fleeing enemy. Suddenly, during the mix of it all, an MH-6M Little Bird that was conducting a gun run for the SOF task force went down and exploded into large flames. No one survived. For Major Morgan, it was devastating. The pilot of that Little Bird was one of his closest friends, and he had watched it go down on the battlefield. The explosion was so massive that the occupants could only be identified by DNA testing.

On June 7, 2006, the battalion received great news. Our recent operations had put Zarqawi on the run and he was now visible for our intelligence and SOF to track him. Battalion HQ informed us to go to 100-percent defensive posture because al-Zarqawi had just been killed by two 500-pound bombs just north of our AO. We were stoked, but we had to be prepared for retaliatory attacks. Our hard-fought efforts had been a success. Finally, some relief, but it was not over yet.

CHAPTER 10

Duty Status Whereabouts Unknown

Counterinsurgency operations require large numbers of troops relative to the civilian population. Some analysts suggest 20 troops per 1,000 inhabitants. Our offensive operations had taken control of much of the countryside, but we needed a 24/7 presence to maintain some semblance of peace. Our offensive momentum was slowly transitioning into a defensive posture to ensure stability and security.

Major Morgan spent a lot of time with the company commanders as they tried to transition to a stable and secure defensive posture for the battalion. For over four months, we had fought from Baghdad all the way to the banks of the Euphrates River, and although it had been a great success, our leadership wanted to exploit it and push forward to pursue the enemy and keep the pressure on. Haycock and Morgan were frustrated with the posture directives from HQ. A plan was needed to secure the lines of communication (LOCs), or roads that would enable our freedom of movement and help strengthen our position for future engagements. Haycock had set the conditions. He wanted two things: an armored or mechanized company to demonstrate combat power on roads, and a dedicated Iraqi Army battalion to secure the checkpoints. He lobbied all the way up to the two-star general-officer level and got both.

The Iraqi Army and a mechanized company with BFVs and M1A2 Abrams tanks added to our combat power; however, they were brand new to the area, they came from the Baghdad city streets, not farmlands and dirt roads. It was a different fight with vehicles further spread out. The Iraqi troops were green with no combat experience.

Since hardcore extremists and foreign fighters had pretty much been wiped out or left the area, we found ourselves in an IED and mortar fight with local Ba'athist Saddam loyalists, who mainly fought for money. They were not as well trained and normally fled in order to avoid direct combat. Locals would get paid $100 by them for a successful strike on a U.S. patrol, which was proven by videos. We were constantly harassed in the summer of 2006 with mortars, small-arms fire, and IEDs.

The worst enemy now was the summer heat. Few can grasp the heat of Iraq. It would reach 120 degrees or more on some days. It just fucking baked you and burned you. The heat was so unbearable that even the enemy did not fight during the day. We were already exhausted from the past nine months with half a combat unit rotating through static observations, sitting in a gun turret, and burning in the sun. Although our combat success helped, the heat sapped our dedication and energy every minute of the day.

As many have observed, hunting terrorists is like the game of whack-a-mole. It was a never-ending effort to find and destroy the latest #1 Most Wanted Terrorist and his cohorts. There seemed to be an endless supply of enemy fighters. Senior AQI leaders would tell their decentralized insurgent cell networks that if they captured American servicemembers they would be rewarded with cash.

On June 16, 2006, SPC Babineau, PFC Menchaca, and PFC Tucker, from our sister 1-502nd First Strike battalion, were baking in the sun pulling a three-day security detail guarding a key bridge when members of the Mujahedeen Shura Council, a group that consisted of six terrorist organizations, ambushed their position. The new #1 asshole, Aby Ayyub al-Masri, the head of AQI in 2006 after Abu Musab al-Zarqawi had been killed, wanted payback for the loss of Zarqawi and had ordered the attack.

The enemy would normally use locals to approach our positions and engage in casual conversation, hoping to lower our guard or security posture. It was not a new technique, but under extreme heat and isolation, a friendly conversation was welcomed by the soldiers isolated on a mission. This is what happened to SPC Babineau, PFC Menchaca, and PFC Tucker. Once their guard was down, the fighters attacked. Babineau was killed immediately and Menchaca and Tucker were captured.

When the report came across the radio that two First Strike soldiers were missing and one was KIA, our commanders immediately began mobilizing the entire battalion for support operations. Emotions were running high. Haycock was not going to wait for orders from the brigade HQ. He, his staff, and company commanders knew the terrain. Haycock and his Assistant S3, Captain Dan Stuewe, and an intelligence officer immediately identified key road intersections to block in order to prevent the enemy from escaping the area. After speaking with 1-502nd battalion commander, Lieutenant Colonel Tom Kunk, and his operations officer over the phone, Haycock and Morgan went to brigade HQ at BIAP and requested the aviation brigade fly two rifle companies and battalion scouts into preplanned landing zones to locate and rescue Menchaca and Tucker whom they believed were being kept at the old Russian power plant, the last fortified safe haven still in enemy control.

Shockingly, the 4th Infantry Division's aviation unit demanded a comprehensive air assault plan. Haycock and Morgan were livid. Time was running out for our fellow warriors. At Strike Brigade HQ, Morgan confronted his counterpart, the aviation brigade operations officer, and demanded immediate execution. He pointed at the map and said, "Pick us up here and drop us off here, here, and here. It's that fucking simple. Put up Apaches. Secure the fucking area and get us on the ground, now!" Instead, they wanted to spend one to two more hours planning, while we already had warriors kitted up and in LZ posture waiting for helicopters. The aviation operations officer refused to execute without more imagery and planning.

While Haycock was getting backbriefs from his company commanders, Morgan immediately went to the brigade commander about the situation. Morgan was hot. We were the 101st Airborne Division after all. Fortunately, the 101st Airborne Division commander and the 101st Aviation Brigade were in Mosul in the Ninewa Province, which was to our north. Our brigade commander called Eagle 8, then Brigadier

General Michael Oates, and explained the situation. Within an hour, the entire 101st Aviation Brigade were wheels up to pick us up. We were locked and loaded and fired up to fight. As the choppers arrived, everyone was on their feet with raised rifles in hand. It was an awesome show of military might, flexing the pure power and capabilities of the 101st.

In situations where soldiers go missing, commanders have a serious decision to make very quickly. They must decide when to categorize the situation as a Duty Status Whereabouts Unknown (DUSTWUN). It is the step before defining a warrior as MIA. It is not an automatic or hasty decision because the moment a DUSTWUN is announced, a four-star headquarters will shift national assets away from all missions to that unit. It is a decision not to be taken lightly. In this situation, it was pretty clear that we had a DUSTWUN. Haycock, Morgan, the brigade staff and the First Strike commander, Lieutenant Colonel Tom Kunk, recommended that the brigade commander declare a DUSTWUN immediately. Once this happened, within minutes this would be across the airwaves and at the Pentagon and White House.

The battalion divided the AO into multiple sectors and assigned platoon-level search operations. Additional forces at the team or squad level were used to block key road intersections. No Fire Areas (NFAs) were placed over these blocking positions so all units and commands knew the locations of all friendly forces. We assumed risk and left roads unprotected in order to maximize search operations. UH-60s were inserting and extracting Screaming Eagles all over the battlefield. AH-64s Apaches were constantly circling overhead providing armed reconnaissance. The battalion logistics officer built multiple "speedballs," also known as bags full of water, food, and ammo to quickly resupply troops with those needs. Haycock and Morgan were clear: "No one is coming back in to refit until we find our brothers-in-arms. You will refit on patrol with food and water."

Units outside of the brigade came to the Baghdad airport in order to assist in the search efforts, including numerous Special Operations groups from the U.S. and other nations.

Haycock and Morgan relocated to the Gator Swamp as they directed 1st Platoon of Alpha Company, now commanded by Captain Strong, to air assault in front of the Russian power plant, occupy a blocking position and commence search operations. Morgan was concerned that the enemy would go to the Russian power plant and sneak out the back across the Euphrates River. Fortunately, the First Strike executive officer (XO) Major Fred Wintrich, knew the operations officer of the unit on the other side of the river and they had raced to support us by occupying positions to prevent AQI leaving our brigade AO.

We had to isolate the enemy escape and control the situation from every angle and then hunt them down. Captain Strong's air assault into this position was critical because it was approximately five to seven kilometers north-northwest from the ambush location. We needed him and his warriors on a helicopter now. He was Morgan's previous assistant operations officer and knew what the battalion commander expected. Strong knew he needed to get on the ground and catch any fleeing enemy as First Strike cleared northwest towards his location.

The area around the plant was eerily quiet. As the Black Hawks circled overhead and came in on final approach, they reported no enemy activity. On the southern side, the plant rested up against the Euphrates River. On the western and eastern sides, homes were sparsely located with families working small fields and children playing in the roads and fields. On the northern side, a wide, packed dirt road, paralleled by a large irrigation canal, ran northwest–southeast through our battalion's AO. Directly across from the entrance of the plant, there was a steel bridge that crossed the canal and led to a large plain with a village on the northwestern side, which is where Strong's Alpha Company landed.

1st Platoon's assault force moved northwest to the village to question the locals and establish a blocking position. Upon entering the village, Strong and his element got into a fierce firefight. Within minutes, his men had killed multiple enemy insurgents and captured one. Following the firefight, Staff Sergeant Girard located a blue Bongo pickup truck behind a structure. As he came closer to the truck, he smelled a burning odor. When he peered over the side of the truck, he saw dark stains that looked like blood.

Girard took his squad back to the plant entrance in order to retrace their steps because, based on its location, the truck appeared to have come from there. As they came onto the bridge, they discovered dozens of spent 7.62mm casings on the ground and another large amount of blood. The area also smelled like fuel and burning. As Girard's men fanned out further to reconnoiter the area, they discovered multiple IEDs all around the bridge and by the entrance to the plant.

The battalion commander now faced a dilemma. Strong's 1st Platoon had found strong evidence that Menchaca and Tucker were in the power plant. Haycock needed to decide whether to shift more manpower to the plant or maintain search operations in the outlying area. He requested additional forces from outside the battalion in order to maintain operational momentum across the area. Another infantry company, outside of the 101st Airborne, volunteered and was attached to the battalion to reinforce search operations north and northwest of this location in order to maintain momentum across the battalion AO. This superior force subdued the enemy and secured the region.

Since there was a pool of blood on the bridge, the team believed that our men had been dumped into a canal. Within a couple hours, specialized search and rescue operators landed at the bridge and began dive operations, beginning a three-day recovery operation. While the S&R specialists worked at the bridge, we looked under and through every inch of the surrounding terrain.

Then, Lieutenant "Jackson" came up on the radio and reported he believed that they had discovered the bodies on the side of an unnamed road north of the bridge. Jackson was directed to maneuver within line of sight to confirm his report. He personally walked within 10–20 meters of the bodies until he was ordered to not get any closer and wait for the specialists. The call came over the radio confirming that the bodies of two soldiers had been found one or two kilometers directly north of the bridge where 1st Platoon had found the blood and truck in the village. The bodies had been mutilated beyond recognition. It appeared that the enemy had burned and then dragged the bodies behind the truck from the bridge and turned east onto a small dirt road. Then came the worst: "Negative. I cannot identify the bodies. They have been burned."

It was a grisly situation. Morgan was concerned that the bodies might be booby-trapped so he directed units in the area to surround the location, while he and the battalion commander flew directly to the site. They brought with them an EOD team with a robot and additional combat aviation power.

The sun was setting across the fields and the Euphrates River. The battalion tactical assault command post came in fast in order to avoid surface-to-air fire. Staff Sergeant Cruz, the TAC NCOIC, and Morgan stepped out before the UH-60 Black Hawk birds touched down about 200 meters south of the bodies. They immediately started pulling kits out of the Black Hawks and within seconds it was quiet again. I was a part of the perimeter around the bodies. All we could hear from our position was the crackling of the battalion commander's radio talking with all his company commanders. Morgan took charge of the recovery effort while the battalion commander controlled the area. Key to this evening was recovering the bodies and controlling the fight across the AO. Every Strike Force soldier was out in enemy territory, along with multiple other units. Fighter jets were now flying overhead, breaking the sound barrier to conduct a show of force and prevent the enemy from attacking us. Apaches raced over the roads doing route reconnaissance, while UH-60 Black Hawks loitered with the scout recon platoon being used as a QRF, and sniper teams overwatched the men on the ground. All military resources were committed to getting our fallen heroes off the battlefield. No enemy was going to challenge us, and if they did, they would be immediately destroyed.

The EOD team deployed their robot within minutes, but as soon as they came upon the bodies, the robot batteries went dead. Fortunately, the EOD team had a second robot that completed its mission. The EOD maneuvered the robot around the bodies and discovered what appeared to be a pressure-plate IED underneath them. Morgan's anger and frustration understandably boiled over and he began cursing HQ through the radio until Haycock intervened to steady the situation. Everyone from division to brigade wanted information and wanted it now. There had been so much emotion over the past 48 hours that, despite locating our battle buddies, many had reached new levels of emotional complexity.

The situation, however, was now more complicated because we wanted to avoid further mutilation to the bodies by an explosion. Haycock called the brigade for Strike Ironclaw, which was a huge beast of a vehicle the size of a school bus with a 50-foot steel arm that extended out from the vehicle like an elephant's trunk. The vehicle's main purpose was to probe and remove IEDs from roads. Inside the vehicle, the Strike Ironclaw carried an entire platoon of soldiers as a QRF to support operations during a mission. We needed this team to end this DUSTWUN operation and give closure for our sister battalion, 1-502nd, and, eventually, their families.

Darkness had taken over the day and the heat subsided rapidly. Many of us in 3rd Platoon, Alpha Company were laying prone on the ground only a couple hundred feet from the bodies. We laid in our fighting positions quietly talking about how relieved we were that we had finally found them. I remember talking to my team and struggled to grasp how war could get worse after all we had gone through over the nine months. Then, suddenly, a loud explosion and flashes of light filled the night air to our north.

Strike Ironclaw had been hit by an IED on Route Motorhead. Fortunately, the blast resulted in zero casualties. Haycock and Morgan sat back against the rucksacks and continued to monitor the radio. Then, 20 minutes later, Strike Ironclaw got hit by another IED that exploded into the night sky. Lieutenant Van Dyke had led his Strike Ironclaw team through 11 IED strikes over the past six hours. All we could do was hope and pray they got to us safely.

Upon his arrival, Lieutenant Van Dyke passed by the bodies of Menchaca and Tucker in order to get into a better position to conduct his mission. He attempted to remove the pressure-plate IED from under the bodies. At night, the Strike Ironclaw operates under white lights in order to see wires, cannisters, bombs, debris, etc. The lights simply brought a new horror of war. We could clearly see the bodies of our brothers-in-arms burned, castrated, and decapitated. Van Dyke realized that his soldiers were struggling with the scene. He asked Morgan if he could withdraw a couple hundred yards and let them out of the vehicle. He returned to site alone and proceeded to successfully remove the pressure-plate IED.

Haycock, Morgan, and their security detachment had to personally view and supervise the return of our fallen heroes' bodies home. The sight of the bodies illuminated the level of hatred, evil, and disregard of humanity by a fanatical "religious" enemy. It was incomprehensible.

War is ugly. A DUSTWUN is an example of the horror of combat. It leaves an indelible imprint in the minds of those who witness it. Major Morgan would lead or synchronize five more DUSTWUN operations in Iraq and Afghanistan over the next few years; he recovered them all, but never in time. He has never been able to fully come to grips with those operations and the failure to find them alive haunts him everyday.

We learned later that our Alpha Company 1st Platoon captured one of the men responsible for the horrific murder of Menchaca and Tucker. The insurgent admitted to the mutilation and burning of our brothers. He said that after he and his team had captured them, he held a mock trial on the bridge in front of all the villagers and executed the two Americans, then mutilated and burned the bodies, and laid a bomb underneath them. A few years later, a couple of our Alpha Company soldiers testified over a video teleconference against the captured insurgent. He was eventually hanged for his war crimes.

Despite its horrific nature, this operation allowed us to gain further control over and momentum against the enemy in the area. After clearing out the last remaining locations near the Euphrates, the battalion took up new positions along the river and farther south towards the Russian power plant. The plant, now isolated, was the last safe haven for the enemy. Our offensive operations had put the enemy on his heels: apart from a few localized tactical victories, the DUSTWUN was a significant strategic and operational setback to the overall morale and well-being of our brigade.

CHAPTER II

Offense is the Best Defense

"Falcon 3, this is Cobra 6, over."

"Cobra 6, this is Falcon 3, over."

"Roger, Falcon 3, this is Cobra 6. Be advised we have had an IED strike. Two KIA and three WIA, all urgent surgical. A 9-line to follow."

We had heard these same words dozens of times over the past 10 months. Soon after the transmission of a 9-line medevac request, we learned whom we had lost. The Army communicates by battle roster numbers in order to protect names over the radio. The commanders have the same roster numbers and can match them to the names and communicate them to the rest of the unit.

On one particular night a massive blast reverberated across the battalion area. The incident occurred during a standard relief-in-place operation between gun vehicle observation posts. We quickly jumped out of bed and geared up. We got word that a Charlie Company patrol had been struck by a 500-pound-plus IED buried under an asphalt roadway. We learned that Staff Sergeant Bievre and SPC Beyer had been killed immediately, while Sergeant Price, Sergeant Redle, and SPC Miguel had been seriously injured.

Everything having to do with an IED is overwhelming—no matter how many you have experienced: the actual blast itself and having to regain your wits, the site of the blast hole, and, of course, the damage it can do to your best friend next to you. As part of standing orders, we had to "backhaul" any destroyed vehicles and clean them for disposition.

On backhaul duty, I passed by the bomb site. The frame of Bievre's vehicle had folded upwards under the driver and passenger seats. It was almost a perfect "V" shape. It hadn't been cleaned yet, so blood, bone, and clothing were clearly visible. Staff Sergeant Bievre's up-armored gun vehicle was brought back and stored at Alpha Company CP at FOB Striker for a couple days after the blast.

Normally, these sights were routine to frontline warriors, but I never reflected on the impact it had on those soldiers supporting the rear base camps. You cannot underestimate the impact of war on any one individual warrior's experience; it affects each of us individually and seriously. At this point, many of us would pray for courage to bring the fight to the enemy and that God would continue to watch over us and guide our decisions as the deployment moved closer to the end.

The battalion had received guidance from higher headquarters to slow the pace of offensive operations following the deaths of Babineau, Menchaca, and Tucker. The two-star division headquarters from 4th Infantry Division directed a more defensive posture, which simply gave positional advantage back to the enemy. As a result, our OPs and patrol bases increasingly became targets for enemy mortar and sniper teams.

Our past successes had now led to a steady state of defensive operations that could be insanely boring. We had gone from violent combat fighting AQI terror cells to a complete halt. We were used to conducting daily offensive combat operations, consisting of extreme adrenaline rushes while in gunfights, IED explosions, foot pursuits, air assault raids, and even wild car chases. Now, we were mostly trying to figure out what MRE meal would be best, while bullshitting about being back at home or being crammed inside a gun truck with three or four other foul-smelling warriors.

We were 60 days from redeployment back to family and friends. Without the distraction of offensive missions, we fell into one of most dangerous mindsets in any war: complacency. This laidback attitude develops near the end of a deployment when units see the light at the end of tunnel and become less aggressive for fear of getting killed or wounded. We had made it this far, so why risk it, right? But this was war and nothing stayed the same for long.

To deal with sporadic but deadly enemy mortar attacks, Major Morgan came up with a counter-mortar plan for what was now Renegade Swamp, formerly known as Gator Swamp. Alpha Company assumed control of a new area north of Gator Swamp and the Russian power plant, while Bravo "Renegade" Company, commanded by Captain Rivier, assumed control of Renegade Swamp.

Morgan devised a plan that called for the battalion scouts to insert into ambush positions since we knew the points of origin of two of the enemy mortars. It was a good plan. Rivier had been one of Morgan's platoon leaders during the 2003–04 invasion of Iraq and they had a strong relationship. The battalion was going to fly loud, company-level Raven UAVs for 48 hours over one enemy location, while leaving the other uncovered. The aim was to get the enemy to fire from the uncovered area, while the battalion scouts infiltrated the area under cover of the Raven UAVs. Renegade Swamp would basically button up for those 48 hours and prepare for incoming mortar attacks. It was clearly risky, but, if successful, we'd take out both locations.

Renegade Swamp withstood mortar attacks for two days and held on with little damage and no casualties. Enemy mortar fire was not accurate and often landed short. Meanwhile, the scouts maneuvered under darkness into the area where the Raven UAVs flew low and loud. The battalion shifted the Ravens on day three from the area where our scouts had inserted over to the enemy mortar positions. On day three, in the evening, the enemy tried to occupy new mortar points and when they did the battalion scouts simply ambushed them in a storm of machine-gun fire and grenades and killed them all.

The scouts recovered a shitload of equipment off the AQI fighters, ranging from mortar tubes and bombs to AK-47s to vests. Most important, they found a few more Garmin GPS devices which contained valuable intel of AQI locations. The success of the counter-mortar operation shifted our battalion mindset back to offensive operations, but under the guise of ambushes and reconnaissance to protect the area defenses. Since the division headquarters simply did not understand our AO and were unwilling to listen to our circumstances, we adapted to protect our troops and continued taking the fight to the enemy through active security patrols.

Our operations were defensive in nature, but offensive in spirit. We were back in the fight. The battalion exploited the Garmin devices to gain intel about enemy movements by using a man-overboard (MOB) technique. The MOB function is a common feature for GPS units in a maritime environment to recover a person who has fallen overboard. When the MOB button is pressed, the GPS automatically marks a waypoint at the current location and allows you to enable a "go to" navigation line to take you back to the initiated MOB location. In these devices, you can also use the MOB capability to determine the history of waypoints. We mapped out the movement of this AQI cell through analysis of how many contacts at one site versus the other. Then, the intelligence officer overlaid them with enemy mortar points, past attacks and operations, and other intelligence data, and was able to then determine the likely locations of cache sites, meeting sites, and key leader sites.

For the next few weeks, the battalion conducted ambushes, reconnaissance, and movement to contact to disrupt the enemy. We were experienced, patient, and aggressive. We now had our intelligence to act on at our time and choosing. Every other day, we heard our helicopters inserting another Strike Force platoon for a two- to three-day operation to act on intelligence from our battalion scouts' success. We killed or captured more AQI leaders, discovered more IED factories, and destroyed multiple caches than we had during the past 10 months of the deployment.

Our Strike Force battalion was within a few weeks of redeployment. Advance teams from our backfill unit, 2nd Brigade, 10th Mountain Division, arrived to do site surveys. But despite our experience and successful mission, we still experienced disasters.

In July 2006, Staff Sergeant Durbin, with Bravo Company, led a patrol from Renegade Swamp to locate IEDs and inspect a large concertina-wire obstacle emplaced by our company to block AQI VBIEDS from reaching Baghdad. Durbin had joined the Army in 2001 and had married his high-school sweetheart. He was a fast mover, getting promoted ahead of his peers. He was a professional and the sky was the limit for him. On this day, Durbin's dismounted patrol remained off the road per normal procedure using scanning techniques to locate possible ambushes and IED emplacements. The patrol consolidated at an intermediate point to discuss the current situation and follow-up actions when one of the patrol members noticed signs of a possible IED on the side of the road. As always, Durbin led from the front, placing his men farther off. As he approached it, he suddenly heard the click and beep of a remote-controlled IED (RCIED). He had a split second to yell, "IED, COVER!" before he threw himself over the IED and absorbed the blast, thus saving his men but sacrificing his life.

On August 6, 2006, Sergeant Vosbein of 1st Platoon was leading a dismounted patrol when they came up to a well-known IED emplacement hot spot on Route Caprice. Vosbein instructed his men to stay back, while he moved forward to identify a crater from a previous IED explosion (often, the enemy placed an IED near or inside a former blast site). As he neared the crater, he stepped on and triggered a pressure-plate IED and died instantly. Vosbein had been a police officer who gave up a comfortable civilian life to fight in the Global War on Terror. He was a patriot who, like many others, had left his civilian job to serve his country after the 9/11 attacks. He had been shot by an enemy sniper earlier in the deployment, and could have just gone home and recovered, but he didn't. His love for his soldiers led to his ultimate sacrifice, protecting his small group of brothers that he had grown so close to.

Strike Force leaders like Durbin, Vosbein, Tessar, Bievre, and many others in the battalion, placed the well-being of their teammates over their own. Some paid the ultimate sacrifice. Some lost legs, arms, and eyesight. Some carry scars to this day hidden deep in their souls. What matters most is their courage in leadership. By remembering them and their selfless bravery, we can better ourselves every day.

By the end of the deployment, the 502nd Strike Brigade had sustained 67 soldiers killed and hundreds wounded in an effort to dislodge Al-Qaeda fighters from southwest Baghdad and reduce terrorist attacks on the city and its innocent people. We had killed and captured over 100 bombmakers, money men, and terrorist leaders, uncovered over 4,200 IEDs, and 120 weapon caches. Our persistence and exhaustive efforts contributed greatly to the mission to secure the city and help save innocent lives.

But we had also made an impact on the hearts and minds of the people beleaguered by war. We had helped train two Iraqi Army brigades. We helped build new schools, roads, bridges, power plants, and re-established electricity for the region. The local populace seemed visibly freer; it was now safer for them to walk down the road, allow their children to play and to go to school, and to go about their daily lives without fear. Most important, Iraqi citizens were able to vote for their government without the stifling fear of retribution for the first time in their lives. The fight, however, was far from over despite our efforts.

CHAPTER 12

Battalion Scout Reconnaissance/ Sniper Platoon

By late 2006, my first deployment was done and we returned home. Flight attendants walked up and down the aisles of the commercial flight waking up exhausted soldiers still in their combat uniforms. I looked over from the center of the aircraft and saw my brothers-in-arms lifting up the window shades and crowding each other to see Fort Campbell. Soon, the huge aircraft would end its journey from Baghdad through Kuwait and Ireland to the home of the Screaming Eagles in Kentucky.

In typical military fashion, we were told what was going to happen and what we were going to do next. We exited the aircraft and watched the hangar doors open. We then marched into a roaring crowd of families and veterans from World War II, Korea, Vietnam, and *Desert Storm*, many holding signs and yelling their loved ones' names. After 15 minutes of comments from a couple senior leaders on the base, the families surged forward from the stands to meet their returning warriors.

What I loved about that moment was not just that I saw my family, but I got to see senior officers to privates being absorbed in the arms of their loved ones. It was extremely special to see warriors, who had fought so violently and bravely in combat, now so vulnerable with their families. The initial embrace with family was overwhelming because it made me realize how fortunate I was to be alive and back with my loved ones in America. However, over the following days, I began to realize how crazy everything had been. For the first time, I was alone among my family without a shared experience and it was difficult to process internally and discuss openly. I was living in two worlds—one was combat and fear and the other was family and safety.

The Army issued 30-day vacations to all units following a return from a deployment. It was considered adequate to rest and refit before returning to work. After 12 months in combat and 30 days away from my brothers-in-arms, I wanted to get back to them because it was a familiar environment. It was what I had known for a year. I felt at ease among my fellow soldiers. In November 2006, our 30-day vacation ended and the training tempo simply picked right back up like it was 2005. Every unit across the Army was on rotational deployments. Some of us never got a break. Others had had enough and were ready to go tackle their civilian endeavors after courageously serving their country. That's what the American military is all about: volunteering to serve, fighting to protect your country and liberty alongside your fellow warriors, then, hopefully returning to civilian life when your service is done.

The Army's first goal was to deal with manpower shortages in the Middle East. We had lost a lot of experienced warriors in combat. Some guys didn't renew their enlistment contracts. Some guys reupped but were stationed elsewhere. Lieutenant Colonel Haycock departed command and headed to senior staff work and follow-on senior leader education. Morgan attended the Command and General Staff College (CGSC). He should have gone earlier, but he'd volunteered to stay on in 2005 and 2006 to deploy our battalion to the Triangle of Death instead. But in less than six months the Army pulled Morgan from CGSC, graduated him early, and sent him right back to combat as the Brigade Operations Officer for the famous Currahee Brigade and their deployment to Afghanistan. He was on his third year-long combat deployment in under five years.

New soldiers were anxiously awaiting our arrival, ready to join our teams just like many of us had done in 2004. The Army had projected who was departing our battalion and had sent soldiers to Fort Campbell to assume new roles. Just like me in 2004, they were ready to be assigned to their new squads, platoons, and companies. Like me when I was a cherry, they wanted to prove their mettle and fight for their country. Now, I had that responsibility of training our new soldiers and preparing them for the guaranteed challenges of combat against a relentless enemy.

Our leaders had a shit ton of experience to coach, teach, and develop the new soldiers to fight alongside each other in battle. Most of us had between 12 and over 36 months' combat experience. (Some had deployed to Afghanistan directly after the 9/11 attacks.)

The Battalion Scout Reconnaissance/Sniper Platoon was looking for new leaders and soldiers to fill their ranks. The guys in this premier platoon are the cream of the crop of an infantry battalion. Many had tried to join this group in 2004, but most washed out, including me. I thought about applying again—this time I wasn't just another green recruit. I had combat experience.

One morning in early 2007, I was working with some new recruits when I was told to see the Alpha Company first sergeant. When you get that kind of request as a newly promoted sergeant, the immediate assumption is that it can't be good. When I arrived, the first sergeant's door was closed. I knocked and prepared for some kind of ass-chewing. The first sergeant answered the door and asked me to step in. Staff Sergeant Bush, the Scout Platoon sergeant, one of the most respected men in the battalion, was sitting in a chair in front of the first sergeant's desk.

Staff Sergeant Bush stood up, shook my hand and introduced himself. He epitomized an Army sergeant. Forceful. Present. No bullshit. He informed me that the Scout Platoon needed two assistant recon team leaders due to the normal rotation of soldiers moving on to other units. I looked at him dumbfounded but tried not to show my excitement. It was fucking amazing. I knew they were an elite unit and did some dangerous work while out in small teams, far from friendly lines and support, but I had no idea what they truly did. They were a quiet group and stayed out of the limelight.

The first sergeant said that he believed in the scout mission and wanted to make sure he had team leaders who would represent his Alpha Company well. The caveat was that those selected would return to Alpha Company a couple years later with extra training and experience.

Staff Sergeant Bush then shared some insights about the scouts' mission and what they had experienced in the last couple deployments, from targeting seriously bad dudes in small kill team operations to guiding company commanders into an area after being there for a few days. They hid like ghosts gathering intelligence on bad guys and passed it off to the commanders upon their arrival with assault forces.

He informed me that he had to interview other potential candidates and would get back to me by the end of the week. I was stunned, honored that I was even being considered for this opportunity, in that there are dozens of high-quality team leaders in a battalion. In the meantime, I had to do a short leadership selection course with current Scout Platoon leadership to prove I met their criteria and expectations. I was pumped at the chance to compete, but also anxious about not making the cut. The pressure was enormous because it was a selection process internal to the battalion and visible to all the leadership and all the 800-plus soldiers. If you failed, everyone knew it. I had been in those failing shoes once before and it stung like hell. No way I wanted that to happen again.

Time seemed to drag throughout the week as information began to slip out on who had put in for the Scout Platoon and who were being interviewed. Knowing realistically that dozens of potential candidates had been interviewed, all I could do was just wait and hope it worked out. Even once Staff Sergeant Bush had completed his research, his selection had to get approval from the platoon as a majority, then the battalion CSM and commander.

I have to admit that while this was a great opportunity, I was concerned that my men and other Alpha Company leaders would think I was abandoning them. I even got some shit from a few leaders there telling me exactly that, that I was bailing on them and one even saying that I would never amount to anything. He outranked me but was never a real leader that soldiers wanted to follow or emulate. His jibe motivated me even more to prove him wrong. For my team, I was just beginning to bond with them as their leader. But I could only hope that they'd feel the same way after losing me, disappointed but proud I'd been chosen by this awesome unit, if I made the cut.

By the end of the week, Staff Sergeant Bush met with Sergeant Sullivan and me at the Alpha Company headquarters. Bush sat in a chair by the first sergeant's desk, showing no emotion, which was concerning, while Sullivan and I stood at parade rest with our feet shoulder-width apart and our hands clasped behind our backs. It was a sign of respect for junior soldiers when addressing senior NCOs. In front of officers, we stood at attention with our feet together and arms by our sides.

We did not know how well we had performed during the course, and I honestly assumed Sergeant Sullivan was going to get selected because of his amazing leadership style that I looked up to. He was an awesome warrior. I was still second-guessing if I had pushed hard enough, or if I had made a good enough impression to be selected when Staff Sergeant Bush smiled at us. "You two fuckers ready to be assistant team leaders?"

We both said, "Hell, yes, we are, sergeant!"

Bush's smile disappeared. "Good. Don't fuck this up. Report to the Scout Platoon on Monday. Dismissed."

When we got outside, Sullivan and I gave each other a huge high five. We were stoked and couldn't believe we would be serving together as assistant recon team leaders in the scouts. We had spent a lot of time training and fighting together in Alpha Company, and somehow, we had both got selected out of the entire battalion, to stay together and continue to lead soldiers, only on a different type of mission.

The Scout Platoon consisted of 28 men who had been handpicked by the battalion commander and CSM. Each scout had to be subject matter experts in light infantry operations which included: reconnaissance and surveillance, sniper work, small kill teams, downed aircraft recovery, target acquisition, pathfinder functions, time-sensitive targeting, weather analysis, nuclear-biological-radiological detection, and, on occasions, personal security for senior military officials and civilian personnel. The scouts were the battalion commander's eyes and ears on the battlefield.

I was assigned to Recon Team 1. Each team comprised a team leader, assistant team leader and four soldiers who each specialized in a certain skillset. My team leader, whose name is not disclosed for security purposes, at the time had spent time in the Ranger Regiment and was one of the fittest men I've ever met. I'll never forget how easily that man ruck-marched with 40–60 pounds of kit on his shoulders for miles on end. It looked as if he was skiing on pavement which seriously tested our team's ability to keep up. Ruck-marching is tough, especially with the amount of extra weight we carried in the Scout Platoon. He did his best to prepare me to lead the team and pushed us in training to levels I didn't know a man could reach. However, he didn't have much time left with us because he was going back to the Ranger Regiment to serve in their elite reconnaissance unit.

Recon Team 1 was made up of some seriously accomplished guys who forced me to continuously increase my job knowledge, leadership skills, and physical fitness. They were all intelligent and physically fit; none of them had any combat experience but we'd specifically sought these guys out and really felt they'd all fit the mold needed in the platoon. Brilla, Sawyer, and Engel were from New York. Brilla stood a little over six feet and looked like a college linebacker. He was strong and smart. He had a master's degree in engineering but like so many soldiers who could do anything they wanted, he chose to serve after 9/11.

Sawyer, or Mighty Mouse as I called him, was smart but volatile, a firecracker ready to explode at any second. But his discipline and instincts under pressure were great assets to the team.

Thin and ripped, Engel was a mature soldier with a great head on his shoulders with a passion to do the right thing. Though he was quiet, he'd knock your block off in a boxing match—he was a Golden Glove boxer from the Bronx.

Finally, there was Stauch, who was from California. He had a great sense of humor and always made us laugh, even under the worst circumstances and could always be counted on when the chips were down.

Team 1 sniper attachments, Coey and Betts, were great guys and a blessing to the team. Both were experts in fieldcraft and sniper operations. They enjoyed their job, worked well as a team and were passionate about being the best. They were true warriors who constantly challenged their leaders, each other, and others in the platoon. The entire Scout Platoon had this kind of mentality. We were driven collectively and individually, which set the condition for what was to come in combat.

Lieutenant Stephens was assigned to lead the platoon. We were not sure of him at first because he appeared to be a cocky smartass, but as time went on his leadership style and ability to motivate us won us over. He won our respect as a tactician and expert in counterterrorism (CT) operations. He pushed us hard while caring deeply for his men.

His ability to ensure we understood mission first, while balancing the welfare of the platoon, was remarkable for a young officer.

In the spring of 2007, Lieutenant Stephens informed us that the Scout Platoon could be tasked as a regional time-sensitive targeting (TST) platoon for Al-Hillah in the province of Babylon, south of Baghdad. The area was a few kilometers south-southeast of the Triangle of Death. It was also on the southern side of the Euphrates River and the Russian power plant. Last, the terrain was more desert than the farm fields and canals of our previous deployment.

TST missions require immediate response to kill or capture specific targets because of the specific, reliable, and actionable intelligence that demands rapid action. This type of operation was normally tasked to Special Operation Forces, but there were just too many terrorists in Iraq and we needed to relieve the operational tempo for counterterrorist forces.

We upped our training regimen by reaching out to 5th Special Forces Group. Although we had conducted operations that required entering and clearing buildings many times before, we needed to upgrade our tactics. Our approach in the past was more of brute force. We needed extra training, so our unit could be more effective and lethal while raiding unpredictable insurgent locations and still remain safe. The Army's 5th Special Forces Group had sole responsibility for the Middle East and were experts at training other soldiers on how to fight. We met up with and trained with some veteran Green Beret operators in a mock-shoot house on their compound where they ran us through numerous drills. They showed us techniques on how to approach a building, facilitate a breach, and clear structures using special tactics and techniques unfamiliar to the regular Army. It was a special event for the Scout Platoon because our prior training was for traditional reconnaissance missions in support of a large infantry conventional force. These Green Berets helped us prepare for this mission change. As part of a conventional force, we used overwhelming force and less discrimination based on our mission to search and destroy the enemy fighters. However, the overall mission in Iraq had shifted to hunting numerous terrorist leaders, and bombmakers with a surgical and precision kill chain. We learned new breaching techniques, hand and arm signals, and tactics designed for buildings, hallways, and rooms in urban areas. Our snipers also received extra training from SOF marksmen.

A couple months later, we received the official mission order. We increased our daily training tempo. Team members were sent to schools and courses such as Ranger, Sniper, Reconnaissance Surveillance Leaders, Air Assault, Pathfinder, Combat Communications, Combat Driver, and Trauma courses to help increase our operational capabilities to win and survive on the battlefield. Our platoon was ready. The battalion was ready. We were heading back to Iraq to take the fight back to the enemy.

★

The battalion deployed back to Kuwait in the fall of 2007 then flew into Baghdad International Airport where we loaded up on helicopters that flew us south to our new home: Forward Operating Base Kalsu. I could see the Russian power plant as we flew over. I hated that fucking place. It had been the scene of the execution of our fellow soldiers and many other bad memories. It was like I had never left.

FOB Kalsu was located south of Baghdad and directly off Route Tampa, the main supply route running north–south throughout Iraq. It contained about 5,000 soldiers and was surrounded by rural countryside, consisting of mostly farmers and their families. There were two entrances into the base. The main entrance was directly off Route Tampa and was protected by Ugandan troops. Around it was a large 20–30-foot wall that encircled the entire base. The facilities were actually pretty amazing compared to the BIAP facilities a year ago. The chow hall was the highlight of the day with an insane number of options to choose from, all under one roof. The gym and workout facilities were great too.

As elsewhere, the farmland around the base provided great terrain for terrorists to hide in, establish early warning systems, and set up ambushes. To the north was a region called the Chakas that was basically desolate and primarily occupied by Sunnis. The small portion of Shi'a residents in the Chakas lived under strict Sunni Wahhabi rule and were constantly threatened and punished. Route Tampa was to the east of the Chakas and the city of Iskandariyah to the west.

Iskandariyah, one of three principal regions in the Triangle of Death, was more densely populated than the Chakas. It was known for its educational institutions and the large Hateen munitions complex used by the old Saddam regime. During the 1980s, the city contained Saddam's nuclear weapons program; it had been a major military operations hub.

In the Iskandariyah Province and directly to the west of FOB Kalsu was the town of Al-Tunis, a one-traffic-circle type of town that housed one police sub-station, a small agricultural college, a large dairy factory, a madrasa (Islamic college), and numerous shops running along Route Jackson, a secondary north–south highway that ran parallel to Route Tampa just a few miles to the west.

Southwest of FOB Kalsu and directly south of Tunis was Al-Mahawil, a Sunni town known to house Saddam royalists and prior Fedayeen fighters. In addition, it was home to the regional Iraqi police headquarters and its northern Babylon Province emergency response team (ERT), much like an American SWAT team. The ERT was a more advanced Iraqi police unit designed to target high-value targets.

East of Mahawil was a town named Al-Imam, which supported a large Shi'a population that had an intense dislike for the coalition forces. They strongly supported a radical cleric known as Muqtada al-Sadr, or MAS. MAS openly talked about his hatred of the Americans and had a close relationship with Iran. MAS controlled the Jaysh al-Mahdi, or JAM, a violent militia group that often attacked American and Iraqi forces. The city had posters of MAS hanging all over town along with the bright green flags of the JAM extremists.

The southern half of the Chakas was mostly Shi'a and loyal to Jaysh al-Mahdi. The northern sector was mainly Sunni. The two groups engaged in an ongoing sectarian war with each other. We arrived as part of the new Operation *Iraqi Freedom* troop surge in 2007 to help quell the increasing sectarian violence and prevent a civil war between Sunni and Shi'a populations. What we were to discover is that we were in for a fight against both the Sunni AQI extremists and the Shi'a JAM militias. The complexity of the factions was mind-boggling and deadly.

The battalion had been detached yet again from the 101st Airborne Division, like the last deployment, and assigned to the 3rd Infantry

Division. The battalion mission focused on targeting and dismantling insurgent cells operating in the region, while 3rd ID assets were used to secure the major roadways and population centers in order to conduct counterinsurgency operations. Alpha Company was the battalion's main effort and operated in the Iskandariyah area to the northwest. Bravo Company assumed Patrol Base Copper and operated in the northeast. Charlie and Delta Companies conducted operations out of FOB Kalsu, where they were tasked to clear AQI from the region.

The Scout Platoon worked as an assault element for an intelligence driven Joint Time Sensitive Targeting Task Force (JTSTTF). These units were experts at developing actionable intelligence that led to kill or capture missions against high-value targets.

The violent extremist Sunni groups had regained in strength since our last deployment. They were aggressively recruiting throughout the region using violent measures to force compliance from the locals. Numerous Sunni tribal leaders who were seeking peace and stability had been assassinated for standing up to the extremists. In 2008, Sunni Wahhabis were trying to establish a caliphate, similar to the more successful effort of ISIS a decade or so later. They were reinforced with foreign fighters. We had no chance of winning over this group.

On the Shi'a side, JAM's insurgent force was built on locals who were deeply committed to the killing of Americans and were willing to die for it. They were harder to find, kill or capture because they blended into the population more easily than the foreign fighters.

Al-Qaeda remained the most dangerous threat to both their own people and to coalition forces. They would routinely tie up whole Shi'a families inside their homes, place a large artillery shell in the middle of the family and detonate it, killing everyone inside. The tactic was used in an attempt to fuel the sectarian conflict between the two factions and shield their own anticoalition efforts. This clearly caused terror and really pissed us off. Innocent families and children were being terrorized and slaughtered for a radical ideology.

The most dangerous threat in our area was no longer massive underground IEDs. It was the newly designed and Iranian-developed explosively formed penetrator (EFP), a new generation of IED. This device was designed by the Quds Force, one of five branches of Iran's Islamic Revolutionary Guard Corps (IRGC) who provided the training and components to Shi'a terror cells, known as "special groups" or hit squads, under the orders of Muqtada al-Sadr, the radical Iraqi cleric. These Iranian-trained groups were directly responsible for killing more than 600 U.S. troops.

The enemy camouflaged the EFP to blend in with the environment. It might look like a rock amongst other rocks or a box in a pile of trash on the side of the road. This technique made it particularly difficult to find. Once detonated by either command wire, pressure plate, or even a vehicle breaking a beam across the road, the EFP's blast would project a concave metal plate towards the target at such a rate that it would penetrate armored vehicles and ricochet violently inside, killing the troops inside. The effects were devastating both physically and psychologically.

★

On December 15, 2007, Alpha Company, along with 1st and 2nd Platoons of Charlie Company, 4th Platoon of Delta Company, and the mortar section from the battalion, kicked off Operation *Dragoon*. The Scout Platoon was not involved in this operation as we had been ordered to conduct recon operations in the Chakas to confirm or deny an AQI presence there. Operation *Dragoon* was planned and led by Lieutenant Colonel Getchell, the battalion commander, and Captain Penney of Alpha Company. Alpha Company was to assist a larger division-sized operation designed to take back terrain and kill or capture 20-plus AQI fighters believed to be in the area of Iskandariyah and farther west towards the river.

As always, the operation began during pre-dawn darkness. As soon as the battalion began to pull out, forward movement came to a halt when soldiers from 1st Platoon, Charlie Company, found an IED on the main ingress route to the objective. While waiting to have it cleared by EOD, the mine roller in the front truck of 2nd Platoon, Charlie Company, accidently got hit by a passing motorist. The mine roller was a recent modification attached to the front of the lead gun truck to trigger IEDs on dirt roads. It was severally damaged and could not continue. Another mine roller vehicle was dispatched from FOB Kalsu, which assisted both 1st and 2nd Platoons of Charlie Company reach their overwatch blocking positions by mid-afternoon to contain AQI fighters and prevent them from leaving the battlespace. Once Charlie Company was in place, Alpha Company then conducted a large-scale air-assault operation to destroy AQI forces and logistic capabilities. Once inside the objective, they cleared small villages and open farm terrain looking for members and supporters of the AQI cell. They accomplished their mission with no resistance; however, Charlie Company found themselves in another kind of fight against a serious IED threat.

Once Alpha Company landed 2nd Platoon, Charlie Company moved into the town of Khidr to clear it of AQI fighters. The lead vehicle then struck a VOIED that consisted of multiple 120mm artillery rounds. PFC Curtis, PFC Milam, SPC Emery, PFC Tenholder, and Staff Sergeant Nestor were all wounded. The VOIED was so large that it completely cut the road in half, preventing any further movement towards the town. They were off to a slow start in an increasingly dangerous operation. After evacuating their casualties via Black Hawk medevac helicopters, Charlie and Delta Companies and the mortar section slowly advanced and successfully cleared the route into Khidr.

Once the operation was complete and the region secured, 2nd Platoon of Charlie Company began leaving the AO when they struck another VOIED. Sergeant Biddle, Corporal Leon-Barrientos and PFC Molina were wounded. The platoon medic, SPC Gindhart, immediately bailed out of his truck, sprinted through the dust, ignoring the potential for secondary IEDs, to search for the injured soldiers. He located the truck and immediately triaged and stabilized the wounded men.

Though it was a rough start, the battalion's first major operation, *Dragoon*, enabled ISF to take back the region and leave troops in place to maintain control. Unfortunately, we did not detain any enemy fighters. Their whereabouts were still unknown, but were believed to be possibly operating, or even taking refuge, in the untouched Chaka region.

CHAPTER 13

Clearing the Chakas

The Scout Platoon continued the mission to recon the Chaka region, to confirm or deny enemy presence, and build relationships with the local population. We penetrated deep into the northern region, untouched territory believed to contain AQI cells, and identified best routes in for future assault operations. We quickly learned from the locals that this part of the region harbored what they believed to be a large Al-Qaeda cell of 100 members or more. We conducted overt and covert reconnaissance operations to confirm this. The overt operations gave us a feel for the locals' general mood and acceptance of our presence. We communicated with them, attempted to build relations with them, and gathered intelligence about AQI movements and indicators in the area. Our covert patrols looked for enemy activity, weapons caches, vehicle movement and routes, and safe-haven locations.

We often stopped and spoke with local farmers, kids, clerics, and community leaders. They appeared to be excited that we were there and wanted to help in bringing stability and peace back to the region. In our last deployment, they hated us, or feared that if caught speaking with us they'd find themselves dead at the hands of AQI. But over the past year or so, the locals had got tired of being held hostage and killed by AQI. Though they wanted to and did talk to us, they feared reprisals once we left. For this reason, we'd try to have most of our meetings with them after dark to make them feel more comfortable and minimize the likelihood of AQI seeing us there.

One of our first long-range foot patrols, consisting of 12 soldiers, took us deep into the region, far from any friendly support. The local population were shocked to see us as we crossed the canals, catching them off guard while they were focused on farming in their fields. They mostly stood and watched us, displaying no willingness to speak with us. No troops had been in this area for a long time. On this particular day, we exited our vehicles and left our mounted rear security element with the gun trucks. We traversed water canals as handrails and backstops to guide our movements and make sure we knew where we were on the map. The canals concealed our movement, but also provided AQI with plenty of complex ambush opportunities, consisting of machine guns, pressure-plate IEDs, and mortars.

As we maneuvered, we saw children following us, looking for candy or just to chat. It was quite common to see children while on patrol, but these children were neither friendly nor curious about our presence. They ignored our welcoming hand signals and calls from our interpreter to come closer. Despite offers of candy, they just wouldn't approach. We also noticed burning piles of grass to our north and south as we moved, most likely started by the kids. Taking the burning grass and the children's distant behavior into account, we suspected that they were tracking us for Al-Qaeda fighters present in the area.

As we approached the outskirts of a small village, the children began blowing whistles. We quickly spread out in a defensive posture, assuming an ambush was imminent. We continued our advance towards the village. As we stepped through the reed lines, we observed women and younger children running into their homes. Prior experience told us that this was a clear sign of a firefight to come. We quickly went from a routine reconnaissance patrol to combat readiness.

All senses started kicking in. In such situations, your eyes become laser focused, scanning your sector. Your hearing gets sharper. Reactionary responses quicken and your grip tightens on your rifle. All the while you keep telling yourself to chill the fuck out and breathe, so you don't freeze as soon as the fight kicks off.

We informed battalion headquarters of the situation and asked for aviation assets to head our way. Battalion HQ knew that we were moving in a highly contested region so they had a support plan in place should we need it.

We conducted a security halt on an east–west road near a canal intersection to check the map and consider a different route back to the trucks, which were now about two or three miles away. In combat, you never want to go back the same way you came in, to prevent the enemy from attacking you on your way back. As we planned the route, we observed a half-dozen enemy fighters in a truck about 400–600 meters away. One of our snipers identified multiple weapons including a mounted heavy machine gun.

We immediately assumed a fighting formation, spread out, and prepared for an attack, assuming more than one truck or group of fighters were in the area and were potentially attempting to get another angle on us. The other issue we had to consider was that we were also inside what was known as a Sons of Iraq (SOI)-controlled region. Local residents in SOI regions were paid by the U.S. government to secure the region and block roads to deny the enemy freedom of movement. We did not engage the truck at the time because we weren't fully sure if they were an SOI element or not. SOIs were supposed to be armed only at their blocking sites and wear bright yellow reflective vests at all times, but they never really followed the rules. The battlefield was getting more complex and confusing than ever.

We stayed in a defensive posture for a short period as we watched the truck speed off to the south and out of sight behind some reeds. We had already pushed further into the region than any other unit in the recent past, even going further than we had previously planned. We were pushing the limits … and time. Soon, we discovered that we had maneuvered beyond any reasonable reaction time from our rear security gun trucks as well as support from attack helicopters. We had numerous roads, canals, and a couple of villages to maneuver back through to get to our mounted element. We only had three options. The first was to go ahead and call it a day. We had achieved our mission. We had gathered some great intelligence on enemy techniques, tactics, and procedures. The second option was to continue pushing a little further west on the northern side of the canal and knock on doors to the north of the road and ask who's driving around armed to the teeth in trucks with hopes that the locals might know.

Third, we could pursue the suspected truck to confirm whether they were SOI or not.

We decided to pursue the truck, despite the fact that it could be a trap leading us to an ambush. We moved about 200 meters back to the east where we could cross the canal to our south and button hook back to the west to look for the truck that had disappeared on the southern side of the canal. We were trying to throw the suspected AQI fighters off our path in hopes that we could get the drop on them.

After the button hook, we split the patrol in half, placing one team up front in a wedge formation. The right side of the wedge was up against the canal we had just crossed, while the left side pushed a good distance out into an open field. The second element trailed slowly in a traveling overwatch position. About 100 meters into the movement, all hell broke out on the left rear side of the lead element.

SPC Rowlands, machine gunner, was carrying his M249 Squad Automatic Weapon (SAW) and was on the side of the ambush, along with me, I was carrying a rifle with an M203 40mm grenade launcher attached. As shots rang out, Rowlands dropped to the ground and dumped an entire drum of ammo before peeling off to join the rest of the team. I too returned fire, unloaded some rounds and grenades into the direction of the gunfire, then picked up and sprinted to our support-by-fire element. Sergeant Spear, the other team's M203 40mm grenadier, was dropping high-explosive 40mm grenades at a rate that made it sound like he was operating a Mark 19 grenade-launching machine gun.

We had trained and conducted countless reps to prepare us for this exact type of scenario. We were calm and collected thanks to the skilled NCOs in command, ensuring sectors of fire were covered and proper rates of firepower were being distributed at all times. It takes extreme focus and trust at all ends. Only soldiers who have experienced a firefight understand the importance of a controlled gunfight. It's a symphony of gunfire, sweeping you up in its rhythm.

The enemy broke contact and ran southward soon after we engaged, most likely surprised and overwhelmed by our response. After a few moments, we called a ceasefire to conduct a battlefield damage assessment and capture any fighters still alive. We did not pursue because we did not want to extend our formation across any sort of distance. We were a small element and needed to stay together to maximize our combat power. Fortunately, we had sustained no causalities. As we approached the abandoned truck, we found radios, load-bearing vests packed with ammo, grenades and ammunition but no enemy fighters, wounded or dead. We took the weaponry, then dropped thermite grenades into the engine compartment and pushed the truck off the road into a ditch where we left it to burn.

We then walked a short distance to a deserted house nearby to regroup. Once it got dark, we set up three small ambush teams overlooking the truck for a couple hours. We hoped the fighters would attempt to retrieve the gear they had left in the vehicle: we would simply return a more perfected and effective ambush on them, but they never returned.

This engagement set the stage for the rest of our time in the Chakas. The AQI element had in the past been able to maneuver freely and prevent Iraqi forces from controlling the area. They assumed, wrongly, that they could achieve the same result with us. But Scout Platoon, 2-502nd Infantry Battalion, had flipped the game. With overwhelming force and targeted fire and engagement, the Black Hearts had outmaneuvered them in their own backyard.

★

A couple weeks after probing the Chakas, Bravo Company obtained intelligence that a large number of AQI fighters would be meeting at the Jama al-Din Mosque. They teamed up with a local Iraqi Army element and conducted an air-assault operation on the day of the event, Operation *Dolphin 2*, using five UH-60 Black Hawks. Scout Platoon remained on alert as a QRF. The mission was to fly the element in quickly, land, and surround the mosque to prevent anyone from fleeing. They would then conduct a "callout" due to the elevated risk at the time of the high-value targets wearing suicide vests. Callouts were warnings to enemy targets that U.S. forces had them surrounded and they should put down their weapons and surrender. It was a new technique because we were learning that intelligence was worth more than killing the enemy, especially HVTs. And enemy fighters increasingly wore suicide vests.

The initial chalk of soldiers, led by Lieutenant Arias, landed near the mosque and immediately took fire from one of the nearby houses. The team returned fire and maneuvered against the house and took control of it, capturing a couple of fighters. The rest of the assault element, led by SFC Zamiska, surrounded the mosque to prevent any "squirters" (fleeing suspects) from escaping.

The Iraqi Army ordered all the personnel out of the mosque which led to 58 extremists being detained. Fifteen of these were taken into coalition forces' custody because they were identified as key AQI leaders or members. The other 43 were held by the Iraqi Army. The operation was a great success and immediately dismantled AQI's leadership.

Thanks to these ongoing operations to disrupt their efforts to operate in the region, AQI were feeling the squeeze and so were ramping up their offensive and psychological operations. IED explosions increased two- or threefold on roadways, bridges, and goat trails in the hopes of slowing down our mounted and foot patrols in and around the area. VBIED and suicide-vest attacks increased against both coalition forces and the local Shi'a religious and government figures. More enemy spotters were hidden near our patrol bases at night to gather advanced warning on our patrols.

One particular night, Scout Platoon Team 3, led by Staff Sergeant Sullivan, was conducting a foot patrol when they came across a small AQI element of fighters laying in a canal, waiting in ambush. These small groups served two purposes. The first was to spot our patrols and pass on our direction of movement. The second was to maneuver on and engage our patrols to stop our forward progress and kill or injure as many soldiers as possible. As Sergeant Spear crossed through the canal, he was surprised to see them sitting on the other side just feet from him. The enemy fighters lacked night vision technology, so were completely caught off guard. He raised his rifle and engaged one AQI member, knocking him to the ground. He quickly got up and ran away with the rest of his team to hide behind some tall reeds.

Due to the small size of a scout recon team, they fanned out and set into a defensive posture. Spear's quick reaction to the threat had saved his team from being caught up in a deadly ambush. It was a close call, but it confirmed we were probing the right locations, using the right formations, and striking fear in the enemy.

★

The scouts continued with intelligence, surveillance, and reconnaissance operations in the region, operating out of FOB Kalsu and often infiltrating in mid-morning hours. We infiltrated deep into the region, an area the SOIs called "the base" for AQI. Some patrols would last days in hidden sites overlooking particular places of interest. Other patrols were only a few hours in duration, where we'd interact with the local population to learn about the AQI presence or follow up on information our intelligence units had gathered. What we found was that many of the locals were being forced to live under strict Sharia law by the local extremist cells. This severe lifestyle was not popular. It gave us an opportunity to befriend the people and help turn them against the terror fighters.

AQI fighters are extremely creative, developing new strategies almost daily. Just as we were learning more about our enemy, they too were learning about us. They learned our maneuver techniques, studied how we fought, identified our weapons, and noted the canal crossings we used. Many of our missions were at night, which we assumed gave us the freedom to maneuver mostly undetected and aided by night vision tech. But they also monitored our night patrols.

Early one morning, Recon Team 1 of nine soldiers, all heavily armed, was conducting a low-light patrol to gather information in an area believed to contain AQI fighters. We stopped to conduct a security halt. During these halts, we'd all come together in a tight circle, take a knee, and conduct a technique known as SLLS (stop, look, listen, and smell). We would simply freeze and listen for potential enemy fighters or locals nearby. The purpose of SLLS was twofold: first, we wanted to determine if we had disrupted the surrounding area and were possibly being tracked, basically whether the patrol had been compromised. Second, we wanted to settle into the surrounding area and ensure our stealth and concealment.

We came upon a canal crossing that we had used in the past. The crossing required us to walk across a small 12-inch-wide pipe over a 30-foot canal. It required extreme focus to navigate a slippery metal pipe in the dark, wearing night vision, carrying 60–80 pounds of gear, a rifle or machine gun, in wet, muddy boots, and avoid falling into the water and drowning.

Sergeant Alexander, one of our two snipers, was the last to cross. He joined the rest of the team in SLLS position, and slowly knelt. Suddenly, we heard a bang, literally among us, startling everyone. No one knew what it was. It was not an explosion. We looked at each other, dumbfounded. Turns out, Alexander had detonated an IED initiator. The initiator is a blasting cap designed to detonate the main IED. Regardless, it didn't work and only made the small, muffled bang. We had somehow escaped a serious explosion that would have killed and or wounded the entire patrol. This was one of many near-death incidents that increased our faith that God wanted to keep us around a little longer to serve another purpose. Like Alexander, who was a devout Christian, we truly believed that God was watching over us that night.

We experienced many such near-fatal incidents during operations that strengthened many of our men's faith. Such an event occurred on another recon patrol, only a short time after Alexander's near-death experience. On Christmas morning, SPC McCutchin woke up and jokingly told everyone that there was going to be a Christmas Day miracle. Our mission was to recon an area where one of our teams had been ambushed a couple days earlier. This time we were taking a larger force. We eventually got to the area we wanted to probe, so our dismounts began walking away from the trucks while drivers began attempting to maneuver trucks into an overwatch position. While our dismounted element maneuvered into lower ground where we had not patrolled in the past, Doc Gilman and I were walking 30–40 feet in front of the lead truck, just off the road, when the front driver's side tire hit a huge IED. Pieces of tire and hood rocketed past us and the other dismounts who were actually below the road. I looked back and observed a large part of the hood literally hundreds of feet in the air. I immediately assumed we had numerous casualties. We quickly ran back to the blast site.

Pieces of the truck were still falling from the sky as the entire dismounted patrol began searching for the wounded teammates. Slowly, soldiers staggered out of the dust. SPC Walsh and SPC McCutchin were not accounted for. Suddenly, SPC Walsh kicked open his door and laughingly ripped off a cowboy-like "yee-haw." Nothing about the incident was funny, but in the moment when you realize you have survived, sometimes the holy-fuck factor reveals itself in laughter. Later, we discovered that only two of the four large artillery shells had detonated under the truck. We were very thankful to be able to live and fight another day. McCutchin, who was also uninjured, was very sure to inform us that he was right that a Christmas Day miracle had indeed occurred.

★

As attacks escalated, we determined that our scout patrols needed to start focusing on targeting operations to kill or capture enemy fighters. So, a couple weeks later, Lieutenant Colonel Getchell approved a mission to push deeper into the Chakas. The operation was called Operation *Leprechaun*, which got its name from our platoon callsign, the Leprechauns. The operation called for us to disrupt enemy activity and gain intelligence for follow-on kill or capture missions. We would partner with an Iraqi Army division and Iraqi Special Forces to take the region back from AQI. The plan was for us, once again, to throw ourselves into the middle of AQI's backyard, forcing them to attack our patrol base or our foot patrols. This would expose their locations, and the size and strength of their forces. Once located, we could utilize ISR to follow them back to their strongholds. All this information would then be analyzed by battalion, where they'd then use the company infantry units to target and destroy the AQI safe houses and compounds. It was a risky operation but crucial to overall mission success.

Operation *Leprechaun* started off slowly. AQI fighters avoided contact with our small Scout Platoon but ramped up attacks against the lightly armed Sons of Iraq locals. They were an easy target because they had little or no training. AQI had engaged in a series of sunset attacks against a specific SOI position over several days. AQI had already beaten us to their positions and had taken over numerous structures from the nearby SOI positions, using them to gain elevation and initiate assaults on other SOI locations.

On one late-night operation, we kicked out a patrol towards the location where the SOIs were getting hit hard. Recon Team 1, consisting of Captain Stephens and PFCs Sawyer, Brilla, Stauch, Doc Gilman, Engel, Betts and Coey, and me, moved northwest about a couple hundred meters, just as the sun was setting. A firefight immediately erupted between AQI and the SOIs as we assumed would happen since AQI was now setting a pattern. The fight was intense. Our team quickly conducted a security halt and planned our movement to assist the SOI fighters by ambushing the AQI fighters from their rear or flanks while they were focused attacking the SOIs to their front.

We informed HQ of our intentions, dropped our assault packs in the reeds next to the canal and, weapons in hand, entered the area as soon as the fighting stopped. We had already reconnoitered the AQI attack locations, so we had a good idea where they would be. Captain Stephens directed a final security halt just south of where the firefight had occurred, then continued moving north in the complete darkness to confirm the status of the personnel inside the SOI position. We spread the formation out into a wedge in preparation of enemy contact. On our right flank, we saw two structures about 200 meters apart in an open area the size of two football fields. One structure was a single story, the other was two stories. Beyond that field to the north was a road that ran east–west where the SOI positions were located.

We had gone only 50–100 meters when a heavy volley of machine-gun fire erupted, targeting us. We had no cover except the darkness. The AQI element was holed up inside both structures. The small single-story structure had an excellent firing position onto our position.

We all bailed into a nearby canal bank for cover and concealment. Sawyer and Brilla, both with M-249 SAWs, laid down a heavy volume of fire on the enemy position while we began peeling off backwards towards our last rally point. A "peel-off" occurs when the unit needs to break contact with a larger enemy force. The lead scout kicked off, firing on fully automatic for a few seconds and then peeling off until he reached the back off the formation. The second scout, now in the lead, repeated the movement until the last scout was set in a covered and concealed position at the end of the team. We repeated this until we had broken contact and reached the canal, with each one of us firing as fast as we could pull the trigger, and at times dumping an entire magazine before peeling off and slapping the next scout so he knew he was next up and last in line.

Once the firing stopped, we feared that we might have accidentally bumped into and engaged the SOI. We were hesitant to maneuver on the structure until we found out for sure who it was. Luckily, we had established a signal plan with the SOIs. We'd fire 40mm parachute flares into the air, so they knew it was us. Then, they would fire what we called handheld pen flares to acknowledge they knew it was us. We fired our flare, then they did too. We identified that we were indeed firing on an enemy location since the pen flares were fired from another location. They were still alive. However, we had just given away our position, so we had to move.

Under cover of the deep darkness, we moved toward one of the structures, using a nearby berm to cover us. The plan was to flank the taller building previously containing a team of AQI fighters. If we could clear and occupy it, one of our teams would gain elevation and fire superiority.

We left one small element to observe the smaller AQI house as the rest of us went on to clear the larger two-story one. Upon entering the building, we discovered that AQI had built up its defenses substantially and had prepped it with sandbags against the walls to protect themselves from SOI attacks. The building had been shot countless times, leaving holes in the walls. RPK casings and links covered the floor. The building was also unstable, so we decided to abandon it and return to the berm with the rest of the team.

We integrated into the fire position about 100 meters from the AQI element in the smaller house. We assumed the AQI cell had assembled in the smaller building to plan a coordinated attack, or break contact. As soon as we joined the other team, enemy fire erupted again against our new position. At this point, we were surprised that they had been able to pinpoint our location, but again we unleashed a barrage of machine-gun, rifle, and 40mm high-explosive rounds into the building. During the firefight, the platoon RTO requested air assets from battalion headquarters. They acknowledged our request and said the attack helicopters were on the way.

We continued to rain heavy volumes of fire on the enemy position. It was an amazing sight, seeing tracer rounds impacting the building to our front, some entering it, others ricocheting against the concrete walls, sending flashes of tracer rounds in every direction.

Soon, we heard the thumping of Kiowa attack helicopters arriving on scene. These Light Horse pilots were extremely aggressive and always hung their asses out there supporting troops on the ground. They were brother grunts in the air, unlike the Apache pilots who fought from a distance. Captain Stephens asked them to recon the surrounding area for possible AQI movement or reinforcements, then requested they drop the AQI house. They immediately located a two-man team maneuvering on our element through the reed line to the north. These guys would've been directly between us and the SOIs. The pilots engaged them and killed them on spot. We were so close that pieces of dirt, debris and probably body parts landed around us. After the quick aerial recon, and the attack on the fighters flanking us, we heard louder thumping, which meant the Kiowas were coming in for kill runs on the building. Light Horse wasted no time and came in hot, emptying their Hellfire ASMs and .50-caliber machine guns into the AQI structure, dropping the entire building on top of the fighters inside. Just like hearing "talking machine guns" is exciting, there is nothing like hearing and feeling the power of our aviation assets driving terrorists into the dirt with their insane weaponry capabilities.

At first light, we moved in to do battlefield damage assessment but were unable to get a precise count on enemy combatants killed due to the rubble. However it was undeniable that we had done exactly what we had planned on doing: pinning the AQI fighters between us and the SOI location to fix and destroy them. We had sustained no casualties. This combat action not only saved the SOI personnel but resulted in the deaths of between four and six AQI fighters and, armed with new intel concerning the enemy control of the area, convinced senior leadership to execute an upcoming Iraqi divisional push into the region: Operation *Nanos 2*.

★

A few weeks later, after intense planning and coordination between the Iraqi and U.S. Armies, Operation *Nanos 2* came to fruition. It consisted of Charlie Company, Delta Company, our scouts, two American EOD teams, a route-clearance team, four Iraqi Army companies, and an Iraqi Special Forces platoon. The operation started with the insertion of a small team of scouts to deceive the enemy into thinking that we were the only patrol in the area and conducting another routine operation. Our team started patrolling areas previously covered, again following some of the same infiltration routes. AQI took the bait, assuming we were the same size patrol based on recent operations. They quickly emplaced a large quantity of IEDs on the roadways, bridges, canal crossings, and dismounted routes across the canals, and then occupied ambush positions, assuming an overall defensive posture. They thought that this time they were prepared to inflict serious casualties on our small team out in the open; they were so focused on us that they took their eyes off the rest of the battlespace.

Charlie Company's 3rd Platoon with an Iraqi Special Forces platoon attacked from north to south with the battalion Tactical Assault Center (TAC) element. The TAC's movement was slow because they needed to deliberately clear the road of IEDs to ensure safe movement during the operation. My team, along with the rest of Scout Platoon, teamed up with 2nd Platoon of Charlie Company, and numerous Iraqi Army companies and attacked right through the center of the battlespace, moving east to west. Each one of our scout recon teams was attached to an Iraqi infantry company. We knew the terrain and helped guide the Iraqis onto the enemy. The avenue of attack completely caught AQI off guard and allowed us to mostly drive forward on foot with minimal disruptions from IEDs.

As Charlie Company maneuvered south, PFC Cook, the youngest soldier in Charlie Company stepped on a pressure-plate IED consisting of two 57mm anti-aircraft rounds. The explosion sent him flying through the air. One of his legs was gone and his lower body was laced with shrapnel. The combat medics quickly placed a tourniquet on him to keep him alive until the medevac chopper arrived.

As soon as the explosion occurred, the battalion TAC, consisting of Lieutenant Colonel Getchell and CSM Benson, dismounted their vehicles approximately 200 meters away and hurried to the blast site. Another explosion went off behind them. They had stopped near a large IED that had been set off by a command detonation triggering device activated by a nearby AQI fighter. They instantly turned and ran back to their trucks, fearing the worst. They discovered that PFC McClellan and Sergeant Jump were badly wounded. Both soldiers were quickly extracted from their destroyed vehicles and treated for their wounds. They were lucky.

Then, a third blast went off on the other side of a nearby canal. Iraqi Special Forces platoon leader, Mulazem Muhammad, had stepped on a pressure plate while reconnoitering the location where he planned to move. The blast completely severed his foot. When the medevac helicopters arrived, thinking they had one patient, they found they now had four.

PFC McClellan fought for his life for weeks until he succumbed to his wounds while being treated at the Walter Reed Army Hospital. He epitomized the grit and true warrior spirit of the 101st Airborne Screaming Eagles. He was the perfect example of an American patriot and defender of this country and those defenseless in foreign lands.

The operation had started off in chaos. Three IEDs. Three different locations. Multiple casualties. Our scout recon teams focused on advising and assisting the Iraqi Army elements to coordinate with each other, while trying to guide them forward through the IED-littered route. While pushing west, we located so many IEDs that we just marked them with bright orange VS-17 panel strips and ChemLites, colored tubes which when broken and shaken glowed in the dark. We knew EOD would eventually come clear them behind us.

Up ahead we noticed two OH-58D Kiowas being engaged by AQI small-arms fire. The aggressiveness of our pilots was amazing. Despite being fired upon, we heard the thumping of rotor blades as the Kiowas made hard turns back on the enemy and engaged with rockets and heavy machine-gun fire, destroying them in place. They were fearless and we loved those pilots. They never hesitated.

We pushed harder, faster, and deeper into the Chakas region in order to catch AQI off guard. Our Iraqi element located a large VBIED factory which consisted of a sizable number of artillery and mortar rounds, over 1,000 feet of detonation cord, a large tank of explosives, several sets of stolen Iraqi body armor, Saudi Arabian Wahabi propaganda, and banners of the Islamic State of Iraq, later to be known as ISIS. In the end, Operation *Nanos* captured over 100 AQI fighters and supporters. We cleared the entire region and left it in the hands of the Iraqi Army. It was another successful U.S. coalition operation thanks to the sacrifices of our heroic warriors.

CHAPTER 14

Keeping Up the Pressure

The operations in the Chakas had mostly ended by the end of February 2008. Thanks to the bravery and expertise of Charlie and Delta Companies, the Iraqi Army, and the Scout Platoon. AQI was no longer a major threat and the region was now finally under the control of the Iraqi Army.

The battalion and local population was now facing a new threat and went back to targeting smaller Jaysh al-Mahdi cells operating around FOB Kalsu and to the south. JAM cells, some of which were Iranian trained and armed, had been quiet for months. Muqtada al-Sadr, their religious leader, had called a ceasefire and his 50,000-plus armed militia had been stood down as he negotiated with the Iraqi government to end the conflict.

The short reprieve didn't last long. In March 2008, when negotiations with the government fell apart, Muqtada al-Sadr turned up the heat again and a new battle front was upon us. With Iranian support, JAM renewed its mission to destabilize the region and take control. They aimed to create as much terror as possible, so they attacked the most visible portion of the Iraqi government, its police force. Numerous police stations were overrun by JAM cells; Iraqi police were being slaughtered and were quitting in droves.

FOB Kalsu was a strategic location and JAM knew it. Based there, our battalion was right in the middle of the new enemy initiative. We heard gunfire and explosions day and night throughout the region. JAM started attacking multiple U.S. bases and outposts with explosively formed projectile IEDs (EFPs). Our convoys on Route Tampa, just south of FOB Kalsu, were being continuously attacked, maiming and killing our troops and destroying our equipment.

The battalion began planning a new phase of operations with the 3rd Infantry Division to target JAM cells. The scouts assumed responsibility for the Al-Imam and Mahawil districts which consisted of a few towns, lots of markets, and a district center. These two districts were experiencing most of the JAM activity. At the same time, we began providing manpower for increasingly fast-paced time-sensitive targeting missions. Since we had previously spent most of our time in the Chakas region targeting AQI fighters and not JAM, we needed to quickly get out there and learn everything about our new AO and enemy tactics.

We first focused on route and area reconnaissance of three towns: Tunis, Mahawil, and Al-Imam. These urban centers were heavily Shi'a influenced and contained major JAM propaganda and support, in the sectarian fight against U.S. forces and the Sunni population. Tunis was the smallest of the three and was located only a couple miles directly west from FOB Kalsu. A couple miles south of Tunis along Route Jackson was Mahawil. Imam was located a couple miles due east of Mahawil.

The people of Tunis generally welcomed our presence. Since they were the closest to FOB Kalsu, they had the most interaction with us and generally received more reconstruction and development aid than most. Alpha Company had to pass through Tunis several times a day, often stopping to engage with the local leadership, and ensuring the Iraqi government and U.S. forces delivered essential services to their people.

Mahawil acknowledged our presence because we spent much of our time training and operating with the police there. The city housed the regional police headquarters. The people respected the police because they knew that the police were trying to secure the population from extremists and foreign fighters. Since we were enabling the police with intelligence, technology, uniforms, and training, the population hesitantly accepted us.

Al-Imam was an entirely different story. It was heavily influenced by JAM. It had a dark, cult-like feeling, full of hatred and suspicion. When we rolled into the city the first time, people looked at us like we were hostile aliens. Green flags, symbolizing unity with al-Sadr and JAM, hung everywhere. Dozens of posters of al-Sadr hung inside local shops and on buildings, idolizing him. We immediately knew we were going to have a tough time winning over this community. Its people were extremely standoffish and would not interact with us.

During our second patrol there, we tore down every single poster we could find of al-Sadr and seized JAM propaganda. The people would stop and stare in horror at seeing us rip up the posters of JAM fighters, many of the posters displaying militia fighters holding heavy machine guns. We'd enter tea shops, restaurants, and even houses to inform JAM supporters that we were here to bring stability to the region and that we would be targeting and dismantling the JAM structure. We informed them that they had a choice: either help us bring peace to the region by helping us destroy JAM or watch us hunt them down and find themselves caught in the mix. We stressed how much we wanted their cooperation in this fight, but they just looked at us with hate in their eyes.

It was game on.

We told people to inform JAM members that the platoon with painted guns were there to track them down and would inevitably break their reign of terror. We were making a clear statement that we were committed to bringing security and stability to the area, even if it meant increased operations and possible violence. It was a tough balance because we also were meeting with local leaders and imams about increasing civil projects, like schools, water, and other necessities.

Many of the village and community leaders in Iraq were cynical about how the Army interacted with them. Some units were great at following through with their promises of protection and support while others clearly did not care about how the locals were treated. Strong military leadership from the top down was required to ensure the importance of community engagement and winning over hearts and minds. Without it, units would devolve into apathy or uncontrolled violence and disregard of human life and dignity. Unfortunately, the leadership in this nonmilitary agenda was not always consistent and our efforts to build trust often suffered.

Our platoon was blessed to have Lieutenant Stephens, who knew exactly how to connect with his soldiers and the people. His counterterrorism ideology was not well accepted at first because of how much face time it required with the leaders and people of the community, but it paid off. His first promise to the leaders in our AO was peace and stability once the threat of terrorist elements had been eliminated. This meant going in hard and heavy to secure the area, often guided by intel from locals. Once stability was restored, we'd engage in rebuilding efforts.

This strategy paid off. A local citizen in Al-Imam informed our intelligence attachment from 3rd ID, Sergeant Calhoun, that his neighbor was a JAM supporter and was hiding weapons on his land. Sure enough, we drove out there and found large amounts of weapons and captured the man.

Calhoun was a huge asset to our team. He was an expert in developing a network of highly reliable sources of intelligence that converted into successful kill or capture operations. The best part of it all was that he was assigned solely to our platoon. He took it as a personal mission to protect us. His efforts, together with Lieutenant Stephens' operational tempo, damn near drove us into the dirt, but they spurred us on to prevail over JAM.

★

In early 2008, we got word that a new JAM special group cell had been activated in our area with the sole mission of killing American soldiers and Iraqi police near FOB Kalsu. The Black Hearts were stirring some shit up and shutting down some major shot-callers, which JAM had had enough of. We were on high alert, awaiting more details. However, one morning, just after sunrise, a large EFP explosion rocked the base just outside the front gates and killed two American soldiers in a convoy pulling up to the gates. Calhoun was infuriated that his sources had not given him enough information about the cell. His hard work to prevent this from happening had crumbled in his hands. It was not his fault but he felt responsible. This single incident led him to taking our operational status to a whole new level.

He doubled his efforts immediately, often getting only a few hours of sleep a night, developing intelligence and operations based on this attack. As a result, he received some good information from a local about where JAM operatives were living, eating, meeting, and hiding. Based on his new intel, we immediately started hitting targets almost every night. We rounded up suspects, but still fell short on finding those responsible for the attack that had killed our brothers just outside the front gate.

We eventually obtained intelligence that a high-value JAM operative, most likely the mastermind behind the attack, had been identified as a previous member in the Iraqi military. I cannot remember his real name, so we'll name him RGC, since he had served in the Republican Guard Corps; he was taking refuge in the northern portion of Al-Imam, a known hot spot for JAM fighters and supporters. Calhoun had dialed his location down to one or two homes in a particularly dense neighborhood. One night we slowly rolled into the neighborhood in our gun trucks with ISR above and attack aviation in overwatch at a distance in order to not compromise the operation. Our civilian informant rode along with us and pointed out the first residence. As we passed the first target location, we dropped an infrared ChemLite in front of the residence to mark it for the second team behind us to hit. We then maneuvered carefully to the second location, which was a couple streets north.

When the order was given, Scout Section 1 moved in and successfully captured some JAM supporters at the first location without firing a shot, but our primary target was not there. Scout Section 2 meanwhile had occupied strongpoints around the second objective where JAM suspects were seen running from rooftop to rooftop, the adjoined houses making it easy for them. We instantly bailed out of the vehicles to give pursuit. The ERT scaled some rubble stacked against a house to get to the roof and began chasing the subjects. Some of us set up a perimeter in the vicinity of the second house to block any further escape. In the dark, the remaining ERT and a handful of scouts began sprinting into the surrounding alleyways to cut off the terrorists who we believed may have been trying to draw us away from the location to protect whoever was inside.

Residents were opening doors to see what was going on. Our immediate concern was that our small teams of two to three scouts per team, running in the dark, could easily be outnumbered by some pissed-off supporters. We called in numerous aviation assets as a show of force to contain any local resistance.

After capturing several runners, we carefully began back-clearing the buildings while the ERT members stayed on the roofs, watching for other runners to pop out. Moments later, one runner appeared on a roof trying to escape. When he saw the Iraqi ERT armed to the teeth, he jumped three stories to the ground and broke both ankles. We quickly detained him and identified him to be one of our high-value targets responsible for the bombing at FOB Kalsu, but not our top target, RGC. Calhoun's hard work and personal commitment had helped us execute a successful mission.

★

Over time, our operations resulted in more and more dead ends. We would receive what seemed to be actionable intelligence and would make a call to the Iraqi ERT headquarters. Then we would link up and execute the operation only to find that the targets had taken off. We used solid intel that led to operational success, but things were not adding up: Calhoun started thinking something wasn't right. Eventually, he discovered a couple ERT officers were dirty, and were informing JAM members of the operation in enough time for them to escape. Once the corrupt personnel were identified and removed, our successful missions skyrocketed.

JAM cells, however, continued to attack Iraqi police stations. The Iraqi ERT were spread extremely thin across rural outposts to gather intelligence and reinforce the defense of the local police stations, and sorely needed assistance and manpower. So, we were ordered to join up with them and began living alongside the local police day to day. It allowed us to keep a close eye on infiltrators and placed us right in the middle of the problem areas. At times we'd literally walk out of the police department at night, move a couple blocks and detain JAM fighters. This partnership also gave the Iraqi ERT access to close air support and other combat resources.

More importantly, we gained the personal and professional working relationship vital to our success in the area. By completely merging our platoon with the ERT, we learned their language and culture to a degree we never had experienced before. We spent day in and day out together, forging a commitment to each other and their communities. Soon, we were obtaining more information from both local citizens and the police. JAM fighters were being forced into hiding by the ERT and our battalion efforts.

JAM would seldom engage U.S. forces directly because of our superior power. However, due to our coalition efforts in dismantling their network in the area, they stepped up attacks on the Iraqi police and their families. The situation was getting hard for us to manage.

In mid-March, what we would later dub "March Madness" because of the amount of chaos and combat we were to encounter, the ERT element was traveling south from the Tunis police station on Route Jackson in their marked, unarmored Toyota pickup trucks. They were headed to the Mahawil headquarters when they were successfully ambushed by a JAM cell. The ambush was initiated with a devastating EFP attack, striking the first vehicle in the convoy only two or three miles south of the Tunis station. The JAM element immediately followed up with three RPG strikes on two other vehicles and a heavy volume of AK and RPK fire.

At the time of the attack, we were outside the Tunis station when we heard the explosions and gunfire. We immediately knew what had happened, which was confirmed just seconds later when the ERT radios next to us blew up with transmissions of officers screaming for help.

We quickly grabbed our gear, jumped into our vehicles and raced out of the small compound towards the fight. As we exited the station, we could see a large amount of black smoke rising upwards above the tree line just down the road. As we neared, we saw that the front ERT truck was on its side, completely engulfed in flames. The other two trucks were stopped in the road right behind it. The remaining ERT officers were laying down fire against the enemy holed up in a group of houses about 100 yards away. We came to a quick stop just behind the last ERT truck where we bailed out and took up positions alongside the ERT. The ammunition and explosives in the lead truck were exploding, sending shrapnel flying past us.

Six ERT officers had been killed in the explosion with another three or four severely wounded. Pieces of human body parts littered the road and the air was full of the screams of those laying on the road, yelling for help in Arabic, badly burned and missing arms and legs. Some of them were still on fire. It was surreal.

The firefight stopped within seconds of our arrival on scene, but we had to assume JAM were preparing for another assault. We learned of the enemy composition and location after linking up with the ERT commander. Lieutenant Stephens soon reconfirmed this: JAM fighters were holed up inside the small compound east of the road. We needed to clear the buildings in order to get medevac helicopters on scene. Without hesitation, I grabbed Team 1 and we maneuvered in on the compound while the rest of the scouts began treating the wounded and identifying the dead.

We quickly cleared two of the three structures, finding expended ammunition, but no enemy fighters. We flanked the last house, which was surrounded by farm fields, and prepared for an assault. We knew they had to be in there because it was the last house. We tried to enter through the rear metal door, but it was locked. The next best option was to breach it with a 12-gauge Mossberg 500 shotgun while simultaneously throwing flashbangs on the roof and into adjoining rooms through the windows. Numerous bangs filled the air. The single shotgun blast destroyed the lock and with a reverse donkey kick by Sergeant Ammerman, the door swung open and we quickly cleared the structure to the top floor. Reaching the top, we observed five or six men running southeast away from the scene. They had to cross an open field a couple hundred yards in length to reach a nearby palm grove to gain cover.

We asked for permission to engage the subjects. The ROE strictly stated we could not engage someone unless we knew for certain they were armed or had just engaged coalition forces and were positively identified as the attackers. We couldn't positively identify if they had weapons or were even the people who had attacked the ERT, although all indicators pointed to it. They appeared to be middle-aged males running from an ambush site without any children or women with them. Since we couldn't identify them as clear combatants, I was concerned that they might be innocent residents fleeing the attack for fear of their lives. It wouldn't be the first time that something like this had happened, so

I had to be precise in my judgement or face potential court martial for failure to follow the rules. It was one of the most challenging situations I had found myself in as a leader. I reluctantly denied the men's request to fire on them even though everything in my heart and soul screamed to allow the men to engage and kill them. The team was extremely pissed off, but complied.

We left a small element on the rooftops to provide overwatch and called in the medevac helicopters. I walked back to the destroyed pickup truck and will never forget seeing one of ERT officers inside, still burning. He was burnt so badly that his skin and clothing were completely gone. Many other ERT members were spread all over the road. Despite our best efforts, we had no choice but to step on bones and body parts to try and keep the living alive. It was a scene from a horror movie, but we saved lives, even though six had died.

The fellow ERT teammates were furious, torn apart with emotion. Some were firing their automatic weapons in the air, while screaming at the top of their lungs and crying "Why?" in Arabic. They had just sustained the worst single attack this group had endured up to this point in the war. We did our best to console them. Many of us had been there before and knew the pain they were feeling. Some of our younger scouts had never seen anything like this but performed flawlessly. These 18-to 20-year-old soldiers were fearless in leading Iraqi troops in a mass casualty event while calling in medical support and defending our location. I was extremely proud of them.

Our support of our ERT brothers on that day brought our two units even closer together. We had now truly fought together and died together. Nothing will bring soldiers closer than events like that. The Iraqi ERT increased its dedication to hunt down those responsible and dismantle other JAM cells. They had previously joked that the guys we were hunting were not that bad, just thugs and criminals stirring the pot. After this event, they realized American intelligence was right. We were hunting murderers and killers. They were completely on board now. Anyone in their team who wasn't on board was tossed out. They were now all in. Every operation from that point on was a challenge to restrain them when getting close to a target in order to do it by the numbers. They just wanted to rush in, kick ass, and take names. We were soon in the backseat watching them execute operations against JAM. They were in the lead, protecting their community, fellow citizens and country.

The enemy kept popping up, mainly because we could not be everywhere. Our time-sensitive targeting operations against JAM and AQI disrupted their efforts in the region, but it didn't shut them down. The ERT continued to have a tremendous impact against JAM cells, but it came at a cost. When we took control of one town, the enemy simply dispersed to a safer one. It was a deadly game of cat and mouse with no end in sight. The infantry companies were battling the same issue.

★

In April 2008, our intel indicated that a JAM special group had relocated to an extreme northeastern portion of the Chakas, allowing them to launch attacks directly into eastern Baghdad. Charlie Company requested that our Scout Platoon conduct surveillance over one of the numerous villages for a few days to confirm or deny their presence. The information we gathered was key to the plan for yet another large Iraqi Army assault.

We split the platoon in half in order to keep a low profile during our movement in. The first section of scouts consisted of Recon Team 3, SFC Thornhill, who was our current platoon sergeant, and the snipers. I was in the section consisting of Recon Teams 1 and 2, along with Lieutenant Stephens. The plan was for our section to hang back approximately 15 minutes after the first section had moved out, when we would then step off on the same route. To avoid attracting attention, we set off in pre-dawn darkness on foot. Carrying heavy packs, it would take us two nights to complete the long walk to the town. We had to do this because if we were dropped off by any kind of military transport our cover would have been blown. The goal was for us to get settled into hide sites near the Tigris River for another couple days to overwatch key road intersections and structures.

At least that was the plan, but the enemy had other ideas.

Approximately a mile outside the base, as Section 1 was slowly advancing in a single-file formation, they were ambushed by a 12-man JAM special group cell that was set up in a two-complex compound approximately 100 meters to their south. The fighters laid down a heavy volume of RPK and AK fire. Sergeant Spear radioed, "Contact! Contact! Contact!" Upon hearing the gunfight and the radio transmissions, Lieutenant Stephens immediately ordered us to drop our rucks and unneeded gear and to rush to the action. Staff Sergeant Arnold, Recon Team 2's team leader, led our section in a sprint to assist our brothers.

Section 1 immediately turned towards the threat and returned a heavy volume of fire on the enemy, quickly gaining fire superiority. Sergeant Spear and Corporal Ammerman saturated the northern-side structure with a heavy dose of 40mm high-explosive M203 rounds. As soon as Section 2 arrived, our heavy weapons team dropped down with the rest of Section 1 to assist with a solid base of fire from the north and northwest.

The 12-plus fighters on the roof soon stopped firing and attempted to break contact and run. A portion of Section 1, led by Sergeant Spear, led the assault into the first structure where I took a small team in with them to support his numbers give us a better advantage. We quickly cleared the first floor and maneuvered up the stairs where all the firing had been coming from. Upon reaching the landing on the top floor, we found a middle-aged male laying in the doorway to the roof with mortal wounds to the side of his upper torso from a 40mm grenade strike. He had been running inside the building when a round struck directly beside him. As he struggled to breathe, we attempted to get his name and affiliation. He died right there looking up at us standing over him. He was wearing a load-bearing vest packed with ammunition. Directly beside him was his AK-47 and a radio that was full of chatter in Arabic saying that reinforcements were coming. We immediately called for air support, assuming more fighters were on the way.

While standing on the roof looking for the other fighters, we learned that the rest of the group, consisting of 11 fighters, were in the building to our south only 20 yards away, inside the same compound. We could hear them yelling on their radios asking where their reinforcements were. We quickly occupied a strong point on the roof facing south to look down on the building, while the rest of the team moved into a perimeter around it. Once we were in place, I ordered our interpreter to shout at them to come out unarmed and walk into the courtyard between the two buildings. They immediately yelled back at us in defiance, cussing and swearing. They were completely hidden inside the darkness of the building, refusing to come out because they believed we'd execute them if they did. We continued yelling back and forth for a couple minutes until we eventually threatened them by saying we'd fire explosives into the building and drop it on top of them if they didn't come out.

Eventually two Apache helicopters arrived on scene and helped set the tone by firing Hellfire ASMs into the nearby terrain to show them we were serious. After that, members of the group slowly started coming out. We ordered them to lift their shirts to prove they weren't armed or wrapped in suicide vests, and then had them lay down on the ground. Our contact team then moved in, cleared the building, and detained them all as we covered their movement from the roof. We had just started to conduct tactical questioning when, fortunately, the Charlie Company QRF arrived on scene with the Iraqi police to take over.

We learned from our Iraqi partners that the dead JAM special group fighter upstairs was the leader and had been an Iranian-trained commander and the son of the local imam. We quickly consolidated and continued the mission, leaving Charlie Company to handle the aftermath. We heard later that when Charlie Company returned the remains of the JAM leader to his family, they attempted to explain the situation to the father, but the imam refused to believe that his son had attacked U.S. forces. After a tense encounter, Charlie Company dropped the body off on the front step and told him to piss off too. He clearly didn't support the government's willingness to bring peace to the region and had raised an Iranian-trained terrorist.

We were way behind our time schedule and had to make up a couple kilometers fast, while we still had some darkness to conceal our movement. We also knew other bad guys were in the area after hearing the radio chatter, so it was a tough balance between speed and stealth. What made matters worse was that a dust storm, known as a shamal, was coming. While it could shield us from enemy spotters, it would make travel almost impossible. We decided to slip into an old unoccupied structure while we waited out the storm throughout the day and then picked up for a second night movement.

Around midnight, we started out northeast towards the Tigris River. However, our route unexpectedly took us into a swamp. We found our entire element, knee to waist in mud and water. With each of us was carrying over 65 pounds of gear, including a Kevlar body vest and weapon, each step in the murky water caused our boots to sink even further into the mud. Our M240B machine gunner, SPC McCutchin, then stepped into a hole, fell forward and disappeared underwater. Training kicked in to protect his weapon: all we could see was him holding the gun straight up and out of the water. Another scout quickly grabbed the gun and pulled him up and back above the surface.

We were in a shit sandwich. We were wet and our saturated rucksacks easily weighed nearer 100 pounds. We were in a swamp with absolutely no cover and making a shitload of noise by splashing and cursing as we tried to regain our footing. We'd really be in trouble if we got into a firefight. It took over an hour and damn near pushed us to our physical limits before we covered the 300 or 400 meters out of the swamp. We conducted a halt to listen for any activity, account for our weapons and night vision equipment, and catch our breath. Then, we were off again.

We pushed as hard and as fast as we could through the night, but failed to make it to our objective before sunrise. The sun was coming up and we needed a hide site for yet another day until we could finish the rest of our movement the following night. The only option was a small group of palm trees just off a main roadway.

On our way to the palm grove, we were spotted by a couple locals in a nearby house. We had to decide whether to take the family hostage and occupy their house or continue to the palm trees. If we did not occupy the house and effectively hold them hostage, we risked that the family would inform other local or JAM leadership that were in the area. Decisions like this in combat always involve risk. We collectively chose to hide in the palm grove because, if we took a family hostage, someone would soon enough know they were missing in this type of denser population. It was much different than the area in 2005, when we could take a rural house over and hold the residents there until sunrise.

We quickly settled into a circular defensive perimeter, each point having two soldiers and assigned a sector of fire to overwatch. Our gunners broke down their weapons one at a time in order to clean them while their partners looked outward for any threats. Spear's team and my team took up positions side by side, as we laid out high-explosive rounds and magazines of ammunition in front of us so we could reload rapidly should we come under attack.

SPC Martinez, our RTO, was running the radio for Lieutenant Stephens but was having issues contacting battalion HQ. Nothing was getting through to command or our infantry company CPs. Meanwhile, soon after sunrise, we observed a couple of middle-aged males pointing towards our location. Just beyond them was our objective, the village where we were to conduct surveillance.

We quickly went to 100-percent security, believing the subjects could be spotters for JAM. We were on full alert. We then observed a second set of military-aged males on a rooftop looking towards us from the southeast. It only got worse. Six to eight small pickups packed full of armed men about 300 meters out from our position rolled west and set up perimeter. We were completely surrounded by armed militia. Martinez vigorously attempted to request air assets using numerous radio platforms but without success. We believed we were in serious trouble.

Suddenly, one of the armed males slowly walked towards us through an open field. The rest of his group watched with weapons prepped to engage. He walked the 300 meters or so with his AK-47 at his side. Once he got to within approximately 25 meters, a couple of us slowly raised up out of the foliage with weapons pointing at him, ordering him in Arabic to stop. We identified ourselves as U.S. troops and informed him that we were in the area searching for JAM fighters. We informed him that if he was one, he and his group needed to surrender because we were only one of many groups surrounding the area, being supported by armed drones above ready to strike. It was a complete lie, but he took the bait. He swung his AK-47 onto his back to show that he was not a threat and yelled back to his people that we were American soldiers.

The guys in the trucks immediately pulled out the bright yellow vests we issued the Sons of Iraq to wear while protecting their villages. We had unknowingly inserted ourselves into a friendly militia groups' operation who were also looking for JAM fighters. They had been informed earlier in the morning by the locals who had spotted us, stating they had observed armed men moving through the area, but they did not know who we were. The SOI group said that they had been in the area for a couple days and had only seen JAM fighters on the eastern side of the Tigris.

We stayed for a couple days but did not observe any JAM maneuvering on either side the river. The mission was then canceled.

★

It wasn't long before we found ourselves back in Al-Imam on TST operations. Our intelligence unit was acquiring more intel than ever. Local citizens were increasingly fed up with the violence of the JAM special groups and were coming to FOB Kalsu to provide information on the fighters. In public, they appeared hostile to coalition forces so as to prevent reprisals from the insurgents, but at the base, they felt free to cooperate.

One of the fighters we were targeting in Al-Imam was an effective, violent low-level leader known only as RGC; he'd escaped our clutches a while back. His cell had recently attacked and killed two U.S. Military Police officers. On one particular night, while staying with the Iraqi ERT guys in Mahawil, we got the word that RGC and some of his local fighters were hanging out at a local restaurant in Al-Imam. The JAM cell there had a solid early warning network of individuals placed on all the routes leading into the city to identify U.S. troops coming into the area. So, we decided to ditch our armored vehicles and raid the restaurant using Iraqi police vehicles. Normally, JAM cells wouldn't run from the Iraqi police, so we thought we had better odds. It was a risky, unconventional technique, but if successful, would be well worth it. We had a chance to dismantle a powerful JAM cell.

Sometime before midnight, we quickly put on our kit, grabbed our weapons, and dashed out the door into two marked Iraqi police pickups. The rest of us piled into private cars belonging to some of the police officers. We laid down in the vehicles in order to not be seen. We left some of our guys back with our armored HMMWVs with orders to bring them up once we had secured the site. The marked police trucks and the unmarked police cars took different routes to avoid detection by spotters.

We drove without incident directly to the restaurant. Ironically, this happened to be one of the establishments where a couple months back we had ripped down posters of Muqtada al-Sadr. The ERT vehicles came to a rapid stop as the members jumped out of the cars on the move. Kitted out in full battle gear, the ERT guys shocked both the regular patrons and the JAM fighters. Two fighters jumped up and escaped out the back of the restaurant. The ERT captured four fighters in place and laid them out on their stomachs for all to see. Although both the runners had escaped, we did get information on one of them whom we later on named Aquaman.

The operation was successful and word quickly spread through the community. The local citizens had never seen their Iraqi ERT police take charge against the JAM fighters so effectively. What really opened their eyes was seeing American soldiers serving in a support capacity, not as the main force. I had directed my scouts to hang back, or just behind the ERT police in order to react if needed, but to also observe their actions so we could discuss afterwards and learn lessons. For now, the ERT police were in control.

As a result of the raid, the "Painted Gun" platoon were seen as trusted agents who supported their police and not the invaders as portrayed by insurgent propaganda. The community was gaining trust in our platoon. From that point on, when we entered the city, people increasingly smiled and approached us to say thank you. The rest of the JAM cells either disbanded or relocated to hidden locations because the local population had turned against them.

★

We continued to turn up the heat out in the countryside. Our intelligence located certain targets and their bed-down sites. Some cell members would create a pattern of movement that we were able to interdict, usually in night raids. One example was the cameraman and videographer responsible for putting footage of JAM IED attacks and executions on social media. Known as "Aquaman," he was one of the squirters who had escaped out the back of the restaurant in the raid a few weeks earlier. We had intel that he was hiding in a farmhouse just outside Al-Imam.

We requested attack aviation to surveil the objective from a distance. They informed us they had not seen any movement but identified one vehicle on site and a canal that ran east–west about 25 meters behind the residence. That night, we loaded the trucks and departed Kalsu. We quickly developed a route and contingency plans en route to the objective. We hit Route Tampa, turned south and drove a couple miles where we turned back west on a small, bumpy road that led to the house.

Cutting the engines a few hundred meters out from the objective, we dismounted. As we got close, dogs starting barking. The Apache element reported a person walking out to his vehicle and then going back inside. They could not confirm if he was armed or had anything in his hands at all. Suddenly, the Apache element said that the suspect had run out the back door and dove into the canal line behind the residence.

We scrambled as fast as we could to the canal and had the Apaches racing up and down the canal trying to get a bead on him. Our vehicles quickly occupied other egress locations out of the canal so we could have a multi-layered perimeter with the dismounted teams, the Apaches, and our scouts on the hunt.

Once we cleared the house and the surrounding vehicles and terrain, we deliberately worked our way towards the canal to create overwatch for smaller search teams. Aquaman had nowhere to go, but this was his property and he knew the terrain. Initially, we formed a firing line and pushed forward towards the reeds and water. As we neared it, our interpreter yelled at Aquaman and told him that he was surrounded, that he had nowhere to go and ordered him to surrender. No response. It was a waiting game.

A couple minutes later, the Apache element informed us they had had spotted a small heat signature 10 to 15 feet from us in the water. The Apaches had moved closer in and were using their thermals at a better angle. We pushed closer, using the bright white lights on our rifles to identify his location. Then Staff Sergeant Sullivan observed a man's face sticking up out of the water in order to breathe. Sullivan slung his rifle, picked up a rock and threw it directly at the man but missed. Aquaman didn't budge. We fanned out and yelled at him in Arabic to surrender but he didn't respond. Sullivan picked up another rock and threw a fast ball, this time hitting him right in the face. Aquaman instantly flailed in pain as his hands flew out of the water, clutching his head. He quickly stood up in the chest-high water, hands high and just looked at us in shock. We eventually handed him over to our detention facility. More important, we discovered a treasure trove of intelligence in the house. Calhoun, our intelligence officer, analyzed the information, turning it into actionable intelligence. Our TST operations continued to expose and dismantle the entire JAM network, from leadership to financiers to bombmakers to fighters.

Everything was going well. We had had no serious attacks and no casualties. On April 24, 2008, Staff Sergeant Shawn Whitehead, with Alpha Company, 2-502nd Infantry Battalion, was struck by an IED while on foot patrol in the city of Iskandariyah. Shawn was a hard charger, the epitome of a warrior and leader. Like the loss of so many of our warriors, his death shook us to the core. He had been a scout beforehand so many of the guys knew him, as did I. It just showed us once again to never let down our guard, regardless of current and past success. The enemy always has a vote.

Scout Platoon took a day off from operations and we traveled to Alpha Company to pay our respects at Shawn's memorial. Fortunately, there had been no other casualties. However, when a respected leader like Shawn is killed, it is devastating to a unit and makes everyone feel more vulnerable. Although this deployment was not turning out to be as violent as our previous one in the Triangle of Death, every casualty is unique, powerful in its own right—no matter how many there are. Staff Sergeant Shawn Whitehead will always be remembered as a warrior who cared deeply for his men, motivated leaders and led from the front. We left the memorial recommitted to do everything we could to protect each other, our comrades-in-arms, in future operations. No matter our strength or record of success, we needed to remain vigilant and not succumb to complacence. We needed to finish strong.

By mid-2008, the hard-fought efforts by 2-502nd Strike Force and our ERT brothers had brought stability and security to the region, allowing the Iraqi Army and police to assume control of the communities in the region. New schools were being built, roads paved, water treatment facilities fixed, a dairy facility perfected, and power was being brought back to the region. The region was handed over completely to the Iraqi government. We had completed our mission and were heading back home in mid-November of 2008.

CHAPTER 15

Home

By the end of 2008, our battalion had redeployed back to Fort Campbell. We were back in the grind again. Now, I understood what multi-tour combat veterans went through psychologically and physically. I had accepted and received my second deployment with excitement and commitment. The fact that I could be facing a third one, however, was more difficult to accept. Morgan was already on his fourth deployment since 2003 and it was only the beginning of 2009. His internal fight was to prevent combat zones from becoming his personality. Little did he realize that he was just halfway through his remaining combat tours. I realized that all of us were in different places in our lives with our families, time in service, and future goals. For me, I was ready for a new purpose.

I had spent over two years in combat alongside the most brave and courageous American soldiers and had witnessed many brave and patriotic Iraqi leaders too. I felt in 2008 that they could keep the peace we had helped them to achieve. We wanted them to live normal lives with their families. I also wanted to be able to enjoy life with my family in the United States. We all deserved lives of freedom, appreciation, happiness, and the ability to choose our futures.

When the scouts returned home at the end of 2008, many of us went our own way. For my team, Sergeant Ammerman took over as a newly promoted staff sergeant with SPC Brilla as his assistant team leader. SPC Sawyer, SPC Stauch, and SPC Engel were promoted to sergeants and took over sniper teams. They remained in the Scout Platoon and rebuilt it from the ground up, just like I had helped do almost two years ago. Soon, they would soon find themselves deployed to the extremely violent territory of Afghanistan to fight the Taliban.

I had to make a choice of whether I would stay in the military or leave and go back to the "real world" to pursue my career goal in law enforcement. My decision was heart-wrenching. I loved the guys I had worked with and experienced a huge wave of guilt, fearing that something bad might happen to one of my guys if I left. We had spent over two years preparing for this last deployment together. Some of us had been together for up to six years and on multiple combat deployments. The idea of tossing in the towel and leaving my brothers seemed like abandonment—or quitting.

To make the decision even tougher, I was asked to stay as the Scout Platoon sergeant, the top NCO in the platoon. They dangled the position in front of me and said if I chose to stay, they would ensure that I'd lead them on our next deployment. I had really enjoyed being a team leader in the field and beside them during the grind of training and combat operations; however, being a platoon sergeant meant longer hours and more administrative work, which I hated. I still wanted to get into law enforcement back home and follow in my father's footsteps.

I transitioned out of the military in December 2009 and returned to my hometown of Cameron, Missouri. I had heard that many soldiers experienced difficult times exiting the military and readjusting to civilian life again, but I had no concerns that I would be one of them. I did what every combat infantryman does: I saw a mission and went after it aggressively. I immediately applied to and was accepted by local law enforcement and began training at the police academy. I did not realize that I had many buried demons that I had not processed.

Despite my good fortune to have a very well-grounded and supportive family, along with friends, and a loving wife, I had some problems. After a few weeks in my hometown, I started finding myself agitated by various situations for no reason. I missed the standards and discipline that the military demands of everyone. Despite a loving family, I felt alone.

I needed the camaraderie of our tightknit team. Guilt and depression set in as I knew my former brothers were preparing for war.

I started drinking in order to deal with the guilt and depression of not being there with my buddies. The drinking was initially an attempt to create a safe haven so I could try and return to the way things were in the Army. However, the drinking only led to heated arguments with my wife about who I was becoming versus the man she had married. I quickly found myself failing her, my family, and myself.

Thankfully, my family, friends, and new co-workers in law enforcement helped pull me back out of a journey that many of my friends have continued down, leading to a life of depression, broken relationships, and many unfortunate suicides. Doc Gilman and Specialist McCutchin were some of my very close friends who took their lives back home after the war. Stauch also passed away during a trip he took alone to South America to escape it all. We still don't know how he died other than he was found dead in his room, a possible overdose. These three deaths shook our old team apart, just as it would've had they been killed in combat. We loved them and always will.

These deaths rocked and continue to affect my life. Because of this, I took the time to seek professional help with behavioral health therapists. I went through dozens of them until I finely found one who worked and helped me understand that what I was battling was normal. I had to accept myself and where I was so I could move forward. I remembered Major Morgan always telling us that you needed to understand the enemy, weather, and terrain before you could fully understand your capability to fight. This was very similar to my predicament. I had to understand everything affecting me so I could fight my way up and out to my family and happiness. I say this because if anyone feels this way, please get help. It works, I can contest to this.

I graduated the police academy in 2010 and was hired with an agency in the Kansas City metro area. Law enforcement has been a saving grace for me. I found another type of camaraderie in being a first responder on a new front, protecting my community and its citizens' well-being. I quickly applied a counterinsurgency-like approach of winning hearts and minds to my policing strategy. Policing requires walking and talking among the community and making friends with those you serve. I wanted to be readily available to them and help them feel safe, while working with them to improve their neighborhoods and communities. In return, I was provided feedback and information about potential crime or issues affecting the community. I would play ball with the kids at parks or in the streets, just like we did in Iraq. I found a new way of building relationships and trust.

I continue to cherish my military experience and the bonds I had created with the men I served with in Strike Force. I had experienced life in the extreme in those six and a half years, experienced things that many will never touch or fully understand in their life. My time in the military defined me as a man and a leader. It built the foundation of service, love, teamwork, and sacrifice in me so I could serve my family and community. Despite the horrific experiences of IED explosions and terrorism, I do not regret that I joined the military after 9/11. I witnessed the most courageous, loving, and devoted acts of selflessness among my fellow soldiers. I focus on how they lived and how they affected all of us in their lives, not on how they died. I am truly blessed to have served in our Army and among the Black Hearts of 2nd Battalion, 502nd Infantry "Strike Force."

EPILOGUE

The Kitchen Table Battlefield

Sometime in 2009, Morgan was driving through the Smokey Mountains in North Carolina at night. His kids, aged nine and seven, were dead asleep. He had just returned from Afghanistan, his fifth combat tour with more to come, and had taken his family to the Outer Banks in North Carolina so they could reconnect, reset and reintegrate as husband and wife and as a family. On that late-night drive back to Fort Campbell, he realized that the trip had failed to achieve what he had hoped. He thought: *Well, maybe we're not in love anymore? Have we have become that Army couple who puts mission first over our home? Are mission, combat, and deployments defining who we are versus who we want to be?*

In 2007, Dan was sent to the Command and General Staff College where he could have spent a year taking it easy in a university-like environment. However, in under six months, the Army came to him and asked him to return to combat. Although he could have declined, the culture of the Army and desire to serve took precedence over his family and personal welfare. He was off to combat in 2008 through 2009 for the fourth time since 2003. He did not know at the time he accepted another deployment that he would eventually go back into combat four more times.

Dan shared with me an invaluable bit of advice he had received from Colonel Dixon Gunther, a close friend. "Be careful. You thrive in combat. This is becoming your identity and personality. You cannot let it become your personality because nothing will be the same when this war is over." This insight stuck with me. This is all Dan and his family had witnessed from 2001 to 2015: living two lives every other year for almost two decades. It applies to all who serve in the military, especially those in a combat capacity.

At no time in America's past have we asked our nation's military to do what it has done since 9/11. The War on Terror placed an extraordinary burden on the American military. The conflicts in Afghanistan and Iraq were the longest wars in our history. Mission, combat, and loss of human life over multiple deployments created a sense of detachment from our loved ones and friends left back home; another kind of battle to keep hearts and souls together needed to be fought. Our families—moms and dads, brothers and sisters, and wives and children—had repeatedly been asked to endure anxiety and loss over the past two decades.

We thought we had dealt with our personal grief and trauma together with our comrades-in-arms, with our loved ones, and with our inner selves, but some spent little more than a year in between year-long deployments, never getting much time to understand the impact of combat and death on their wives and children and never fully "resetting and reintegrating" as a father or mother or as a husband or wife. We identified so powerfully as warriors, letting combat define our personalities, that we never saw that a parallel trauma was happening at home—on the kitchen table battlefield.

Dan coined the phrase "the kitchen table battlefield." It's something that is familiar to every military family. Combat veterans reflect upon the "whats" and "whys" of things that happened on the battlefield. The more we think about and discuss past decisions and actions of our unit and battle buddies, the more we appreciate the complexity, danger, and difficulty of our deployments. The phrase or question, "Remember when ..." results in a full range of emotions, from tears of sadness to laughter, anger, and more. More importantly, as we reflect on these experiences, we discover that we never asked our family how the dangers they knew we faced in battle had impacted their lives. The constant threat of receiving that message that one of us was missing or had been killed or seriously injured took a mental toll on them. We need to acknowledge their struggles with grief, fear, and loneliness.

Our Gold Star families who have lost their soldiers in combat continue to gather together to care and support each other as they fought to survive the challenges of the kitchen table battlefield. Take the story of Nancy, the devoted wife of SFC Jonathan Tessar who was killed in action leading his men in combat in 2005. She was leader of the Alpha Company family group at Fort Campbell. His death left her and their children alone to hold their lives together. She could have succumbed to grief and stepped down as the company family group leader. However, she fought through her loss and stayed on for more than a year because she loved her fellow spouses and their commitment to their soldiers who were still fighting in Iraq. She remained devoted to the families because it was her way to finish the mission of service that she and other spouses had begun together.

The emotional ordeal that families go through each day that their soldiers are deployed in war is underestimated in so many ways. Many spouses struggle with how to manage their children's routines, how to keep them focused on school, friends, and activities, all the while trying to maintain normalcy. They juggle anxiety about their soldier, supporting other families simultaneously, and teaching children about what happens in combat.

Patty Morgan, Dan's wife, was a family unit leader at multiple levels. She has shared how difficult it was for her and other families just to keep their hopes alive during the multiple deployments of their spouses. They would have pizza and movie nights. One evening, the children were watching a movie in which an animal died. The Morgans' son broke down in tears because he related that image to his "daddy being killed." Doing her part too, their daughter, Isabel, spent time with children whose fathers had just been killed in combat. Even though she was eight years old at the time, she knew what was happening and wanted to help. Imagine these experiences repeating themselves in the lives of hundreds of families within a battalion, and across each branch of the military.

Combat fatigue and stress of battle do not reside solely on faraway battlefields in the hearts and minds of warriors. The anxiety of not knowing if a husband, wife, father, mother, son or daughter will come home while hearing of their neighbors' family member being killed or severely wounded, is a major emotional challenge. So many spouses go to sleep alone every night, eat dinner alone or with the kids, watch their children walk and talk for the first time, or participate in sports or school activities without their spouse next to them. Even worse, imagine how hard it is for the family when their soldier returns home for a brief time and they all try to re-establish connections and catch up on what's been going in their absence, only to have him or her taken away by yet another deployment. It's gut-wrenching.

The kitchen table battlefield is a mission of itself and requires its own sacrifice that should never be discounted in the overall context of war. It doesn't carry the glory of battle that so many value about the war experience. Combat veterans in the Army look at the number of combat stripes on their right sleeve. The more you have, the more you are to be respected or held in awe. At the same time, those stripes also tell the story of two parallel lives of struggle. We realize now that many of us, if not all of us, were better warriors because we had the confidence and love of our families and partners who fought to maintain their regular lives on the home front. Our respect for the resilience and love among our family support groups is limitless.

In some ways, the *kitchen table battlefield* is a necessary condition to bring balance to the violent nature of war. It should never be forgotten or casually dismissed because it supports the overall effort for our nation, mission, unit, and each other.

Postface

Soon after the time of writing, the United States ended one of the longest wars in American history, despite the fact that it achieved no clear victory. For over almost two decades, military officers faced the challenge of training their soldiers to be dedicated to this seemingly endless mission and to fight to protect our country from the terrorists that threatened freedom. The dedication to mission among units and soldiers started strong but increasingly got harder as deployments increased and soldiers continued to make the ultimate sacrifice. America's disengagement from these wars seemed the best option to end the loss of blood and treasure of our nation and the stresses on our warriors and their families.

Many believed that when America left Afghanistan, there would be another 9/11 attack. Others believed we should have remained, committed to what we started after 9/11. On the other hand, the Afghan people and Government of Afghanistan had twenty years, basically a generation, to end the insider threat to our soldiers, reduce corruption, and provide women's rights, education, and security for their people.

In the summer of 2021, President Biden made the decision to leave Afghanistan. It was an abrupt departure that shook the country of Afghanistan, divided America even further, and sowed despair among our veterans. There are justifiable arguments on whether to have remained in Afghanistan at some degree of military and diplomatic capacity and capability. The decision and the follow-on execution of the withdrawal, however, was an abysmal failure, and an embarrassment to American leadership on a global scale.

Our tactical leadership on the ground in Kabul did a phenomenal job under the conditions they were given, based on the political objective. However, the immediate aftermath and shocking pictures of Afghans begging for freedom from the Talban was gut-wrenching and brought up many conflicting emotions. Though I never deployed to Afghanistan, Dan deployed there multiple times. He seethes with frustration, not over the decision to withdraw as much as with how the decision and execution occurred. As he said, "We're supposed to be fucking better than this."

In Iraq, the situation is more complex. The Middle East region has always been precariously unstable even before the 9/11 attack and remains so even after our commitment against the Global War on Terror. The rise of ISIS, prevalence of Sunni versus Shi'a tension, and humanitarian and economic instability creates an ever-present set of conditions across the region that can and does lead to flash violence. Today, the rising tension between Saudi Arabia and Iran remain paramount. Turkey, which is north of Iraq, remains unpredictable, recently aligning itself more with Russia for economic purposes as well. The geopolitical complexities of the Middle East contribute to endless conflict.

Today, the world is experiencing true interstate war in Ukraine as a result of Russian aggression. Although Ukrainian leadership, military, and citizenry are putting up an extraordinarily courageous fight for survival, Russia's aggression and likelihood of invasion was evident soon after the annexation of the Crimea in 2014. We can point fingers at the failure to support Ukraine earlier and a U.S./NATO deterrence policy failure. The main point is that somewhere in the world there is always conflict, confrontation, or competition. Peace is a brief interlude.

The character of conflict is changing dramatically across the world where we see great power politics and competition emerging to challenge America's role as leader in the fight for freedom and democracy. Today, the world could be sitting at the brink of the use of tactical nuclear weapons by Putin against Ukraine. We must never underestimate the evil intentions of some human beings and their desire for power.

The sacrifices of our Fallen Heroes and Gold Star families must not be forgotten, despite the changing nature of the world and conflict. It is the selflessness of service to our country and its values, and each other that will continue to grow from generation to generation to ensure stability and security. As we move forward, we must continue to honor the last full measure of our Fallen Heroes' devotion to duty in the past, present, and future.

The Black Hearts of 2-502nd Infantry continue to fight, advise and assist allied and partnered forces across the world. The Strike Force battalion transitioned from the high-intensity combat force it was at its inception to one trained to execute counterinsurgency and counterterrorism operations throughout the world.

In late 2013, Strike Force soldiers provided security training and assistance and offensive operations in support of the Iraqi and Afghan security forces. They deployed back to Iraq in 2016 to train and assist the Kurdish Peshmerga forces in the fight against ISIS. In 2019, the Black Hearts conducted security force assistance in Ukraine to advise and assist the Ukrainian armed forces. They developed a joint multinational training group for officers and NCOs, built firing ranges and other training sites, and created a training curriculum to help Ukraine defend itself from Russian aggression.

In 2019, elements of the 502nd Strike Brigade deployed to Africa where they trained and advised the African Response Force in Djibouti. Elsewhere in Africa, elements of Strike Force deployed to Addis Ababa, Ethiopia, to lead a U.S. Army and African Union (AU) joint military exercise called Justified Accord. The exercise enhanced the peacekeeping capability of participating forces from the African Union Mission in Somalia, consisting of over 1,000 troops from Brazil, Burundi, Canada, Djibouti, Ethiopia, France, Italy, the Netherlands, Somalia, Uganda, the United Kingdom, and the United States.

Today, the Black Hearts continue to not only be a national force multiplier, but an internationally recognized fighting unit, committed to excellence in battle. The battalion is modernizing with manned and unmanned weapons systems using artificial intelligence for future combat against adversaries such as China and Russia. They are a well-prepared force that stands ready to fight; they are one of the finest in military history. They carry on their great tradition to protect America from harm today because of the generation of warriors who gave their lives on the battlefields of post-9/11 in Iraq and Afghanistan.

Regardless of politics or the ultimate geopolitical outcomes of these wars, this book only hopes to herald the fact that our Fallen Heroes did not fight and die in vain. While every war is different, no other generation of American warriors has been called upon to deploy and redeploy for over two decades to fight a war. Our generation is the 9/11 Generation of Warriors. Like those before us, we fought for each other and for love of country. We must remember our Fallen Heroes in how they lived, for their loss was not in vain. We also remember those who were wounded along the way and all invisible and visible scars of combat. Finally, we remember our Gold Star families as brave, loving, patriotic, and strong. They live in our hearts and minds because they touch all of us in their special way.

APPENDIX

In Memoriam

God speed to our Fallen Heroes and their Gold Star Families and all those who were wounded and served in Strike Force, the 101st Airborne Division (Air Assault) Screaming Eagles, and in all U.S. forces. You will never be forgotten.

Invasion of Iraq 2003

SGT Brett Christian
SPC Ray Hutchinson
PFC Brandon Oberleitner

Operation *Iraqi Freedom* 2005–2006

SFC Jonathan Tessar
SFC Shawn Dostie
SFC Clarence McSwain
SSG Aram Bass
SSG Jerry Durbin
SSG Santiago Halsel
SSG Mario Bievre
SGT William Meeuwsen
SGT Matthew Vosbein
SPC William Byler
SPC Allen Knop
SPC Sergio Mercedes-Saez

PFC Adam Johnson
PFC David Martin
PFC Adam Shephard
PFC Angelo Zawaydeh
PFC Paul Beyer
PFC Travis Zimmerman
PVT Joshua Powers
PVT Brian Kubik

Operation *Iraqi Freedom* 2007–2008

SSG Shaun Whitehead
SPC William McClellan
SPC Shane Penley

Operation *Enduring Freedom* 2010–2011

SGT Aaron Kramer
SSG Adam Dickmyer
SPC Brett Land
SPC Jacob Carroll
CPL Jacob Carver
SSG Juan Rivadeneira
SSG Sean Flannery
SPC William Middleton
CPL Sean Collins
SPC Patrick Deans
CPL Willie McLawhorn Jr.
SPC Kenneth Necochea
SPC Derek Simonetta
SPC Jorge Villacis
CPL Brandon Kirton

Operation *Inherent Resolve* 2016

1LT Jeffrey Cooper